**Dedicated to the
Sacred Heart of Jesus**

St. Therese with Her Father

# Table of Contents

Introduction ............................................. vi

Chapter 1. Rise and Shine! ............................... 1

Chapter 2. Good Grooming ................................. 9

Chapter 3. Cleanliness Is Next to Godliness ............. 16

Chapter 4. Care of Teeth and Eyes ....................... 25

Chapter 5. Healthy Eating: Nutrition .................... 36

Chapter 6. Exercise and Respect ......................... 48

Chapter 7. Safety in the Home ........................... 62

Chapter 8. Fire Safety .................................. 70

Chapter 9. Strangers and a Word of Caution .............. 82

Chapter 10. Health and Table Manners .................... 90

Chapter 11. Being Helpful and Being Thankful ............ 97

Chapter 12. Respect for Others and Their Belongings .... 108

Chapter 13. Good Posture ............................... 116

Chapter 14. Household Health and Safety ................ 123

Chapter 15. First Aid .................................. 131

Chapter 16. Courtesy at Church ......................... 139

Answer Key ............................................. 147

# Introduction

"Whosoever shall not receive the Kingdom of God
as a little child, shall not enter into it."
(Mark 10:15)

This is a book about health and safety for Catholic third graders. It is also a story about a family, the Martins, who want to be a good Catholic family as they are called to be by Jesus. The father and mother in the family are constantly teaching the children about living the Faith in their daily lives, while at the same time teaching them how to stay healthy and practice safety rules.

It is often in the family room where Mom and Dad discuss with the children various topics and rules about safety and health. The authors hope that those who read this book will have fun, and maybe a little adventure, as you read about the daily lives of the Martin family.

Jesus constantly showed His love and concern for others. He cured the sick and healed those with various illnesses. He repeatedly preached that we should treat others the way we would want them to treat us. So let's begin the stories from the Martin family and see how they try to follow this teaching.

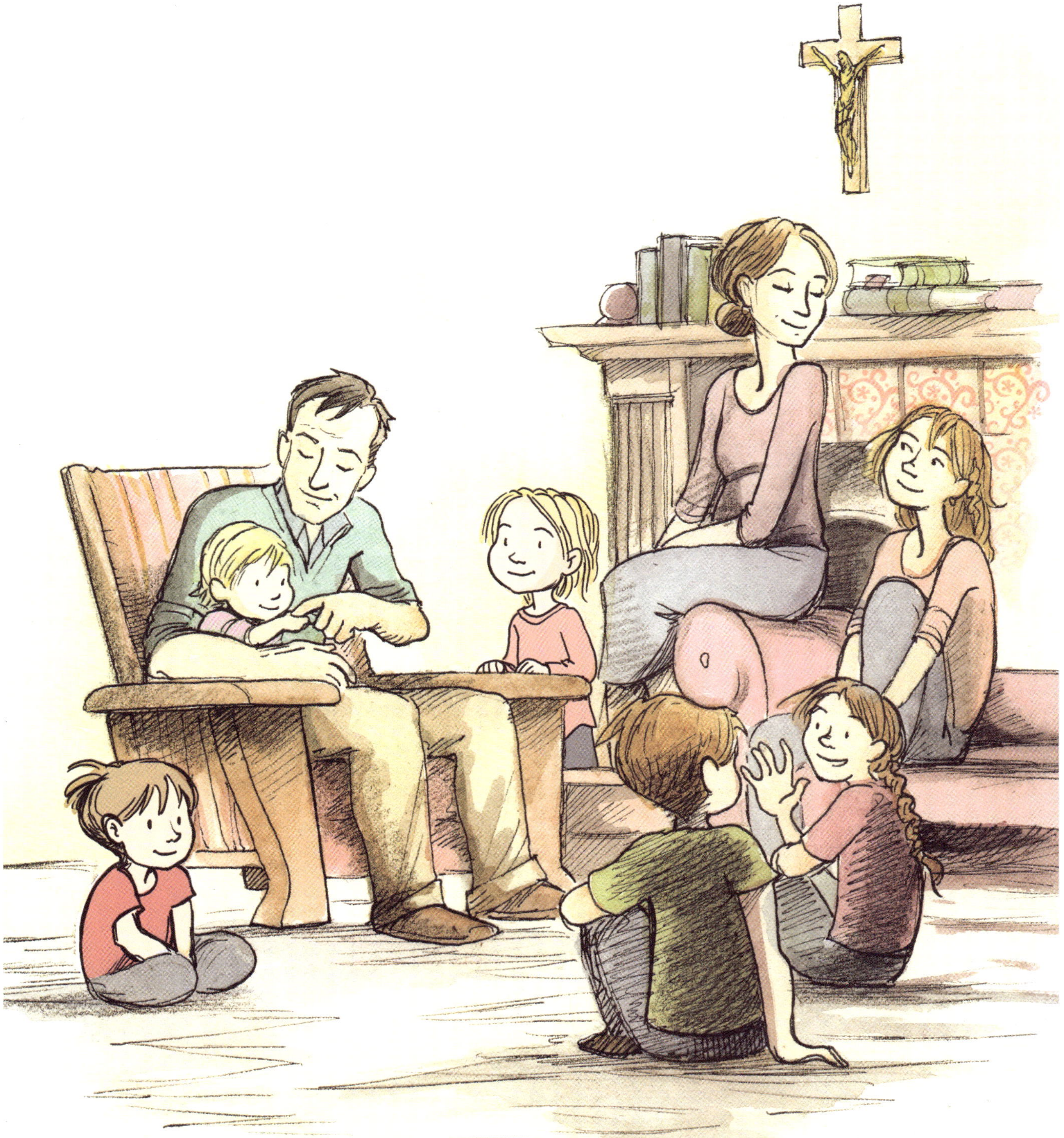

# Chapter 1. Rise and Shine!

The bright morning sun peeks through the window. Twelve-year-old Joanie yawns and stretches. It is time to get up. She looks over at her little five-year-old sister, Annie, and sees her rubbing her eyes. Annie is awake too.

"Good morning, Sleepy Head!" Joanie says cheerfully. "It's time for our morning prayers."

Between their beds is a special table for all their holy items. There are statues of their patron saints: St. Anne sitting with Mary at her side, and St. Joan of Arc with her sword and shield. There are some special holy cards on the table too, and a bottle of holy water, which the girls filled at their church, St. Joseph's. On the wall above the table hangs a crucifix. On another wall is their favorite picture of Our Lady holding the Child Jesus. On the wall over each bed is a picture of a guardian angel.

Health 3 for Young Catholics

J.M.J.

"Let's say our prayers together, Annie!"

> "Good morning, dear Jesus.
> This day is for You.
> We ask you to bless
> All we think, say, and do."

Mother told the children that the Morning Offering is the most important prayer of the entire day. Joanie was amazed to learn that this one prayer turns everything she does all day into a prayer. In the Morning Offering, all of her thoughts, words, and actions are given to Jesus.

Joanie and Annie pray a Hail Mary and an Our Father together. Then they ask for their guardian angels' protection:

> "Angel of God, my guardian dear,
> To whom God's love entrusts me here;
> Ever this day, be at my side
> To light and guard, to rule and guide. Amen."

J.M.J.

When they finish, Joanie gives her little sister a big hug. "You pray so sweetly, little Annie! I think Jesus and Mary must love to hear you pray."

Joanie is happy and full of energy for the new day. She is glad she went right to sleep last night and had nearly ten hours of sleep. Mom said that's just the right amount for her age!

"Let's see," says Joanie, looking through Annie's drawer. "The weatherman said it would be a little chilly this morning and then warm up later." She pulls out a play dress and a sweater. "Perfect!" She helps her sister dress, then she dresses herself.

Joanie takes Annie to the bathroom. The door is shut, so she knocks first to be sure no one is there before going in. Joanie then helps Annie to wash her face and brush her teeth, as she cleans her own face and brushes her teeth. Joanie and Annie return to the bedroom, where Joanie helps Annie brush her hair, then she brushes her own hair. They make their beds, put away their nightgowns, and tidy up. Now they are ready for the new day.

As Annie and Joanie leave their bedroom and start down the hallway, they see their brothers, ten-year-old Johnny and three-year old Tommy, running down the hall.

"Hey!" shouts Johnny. "Did you see the sunrise this morning? No rain! Wow! I hope we can fly our kite today!"

Joanie laughs and says, "Maybe we can!"

Health 3 for Young Catholics

J.M.J.

"I'm hungry!" yells Annie.

"Of course you are, Silly! It's time for breakfast!" says Joanie. "Let's go down with the boys and have breakfast. Mmm! I think Mom's making some special waffles today. I like crispy waffles better than pancakes! I hope we have maple syrup!"

Joanie's mother told her how a healthy breakfast keeps her happy and energetic throughout the day. She is thankful that she likes healthy breakfasts with toast and eggs, sometimes oatmeal and bacon, and sometimes waffles and sausage.

The children walk down the stairs, but Johnny jumps down! When Joanie enters the kitchen, she asks her mother if she needs any help.

"Thank you, Joanie. Will you watch the baby, please? Little Rosie is fussy this morning. Sometimes babies are fussy at eight months because

4  Health 3 for Young Catholics

J.M.J.

their teeth are coming in! Johnny, will you help your little brother with his food? Tommy cannot seem to cut his waffle!" Mom says.

Joanie and Johnny quickly get busy doing what their mother asked.

"Where's Dad? Where's Theresa?" Joanie asks.

"You know Dad likes to sleep a little later on Saturday! And Theresa was working with Dad last night on her algebra lesson. Dad was trying to give her some ideas in solving the problems!"

"I hope Dad will help me when I have algebra!" exclaims Joanie.

Once everyone is seated, Mom says, "Okay, let's say grace. I think it is your turn, Annie, to lead us in grace."

"In the name of the Father, and of the Son, and of the Holy Spirit. Amen. Bless us, O Lord and these Thy gifts, which we are about to receive from Thy bounty, through Christ Our Lord. And God bless everyone in our family. Amen."

"That's fine, Annie! Now let's all eat breakfast. We want to finish in time so that we can receive Holy Communion when we attend Mass. Joanie, remind me to wake up Dad and Theresa before it is too late for them to eat."

"Okay, Mom!"

After breakfast, the children have a few more chores to do. While Joanie helps clean up the breakfast table, Johnny feeds their dog, Bruno. Joanie also does a little sweeping around Rosie's high chair. Mom goes to wake up Dad and Theresa.

"Okay, everybody! Let's get ready for Mass."

"Where's my kite?" Johnny yells.

"I put it in the closet last night," Mom says. "Johnny, you can't fly

Health 3 for Young Catholics

your kite now! Get ready for Mass. We don't want to be late for Mass!"

"Okay, Mom!" shouts Johnny. "Hey, Tommy! You have your shoes on the wrong feet! Let's fix them right! It's going to be a great day! I just know it!"

## Lesson Review

1. What is an important prayer to start the day?

   _____

2. What prayer do you say to ask your guardian angel to watch over you?

   _____

   _____

3. What did Joanie and her sister Annie do to get ready for the day?

   _____

   _____

4. How many hours of sleep did Mrs. Martin say her daughters should get?

5. How many hours of sleep does your Mom or Dad say you should have?

6. Why is it important to eat a healthy breakfast?

7. How does it help your family when you do your chores right away?

8. The Martin family includes Theresa, fourteen years old; Joanie, twelve years old; Johnny, ten years old; Annie, five years old; Tommy, three years old, and Rosie, eight months old. How old are the children in your family?

## Activities

1. Do you have a special place in your bedroom for prayer time? You can use a small shelf or table, the top of your dresser, or even a box turned upside down. Be creative! Make the area beautiful for Jesus. Ask your mom or dad what items you may add to your prayer area. Some things that you might add are a pretty cloth, a statue, holy cards, a bottle of holy water, a crucifix, and a picture of Mary. Include a copy of the Morning Offering if you are just beginning to learn it. You will soon have a great prayer area in your bedroom!

2. On a piece of paper, draw five or more hearts. Cut out the hearts. Then, on each one, write a different chore or activity that you do during the day, such as setting the table. Put these in an envelope or basket on your prayer table. This will help you remember that when you say your Morning Offering, you are giving all these activities to God.

## Did You Know?

Sleep helps young people to grow! There are many things that help young people to grow, such as eating healthy food and exercising. Did you know that getting a good night's rest is important? If you want to make sure you grow as God has planned, eat right, get plenty of exercise, and get plenty of sleep!

# Chapter 2. Good Grooming

Joanie brushes her long brown hair often during the day. She also helps little Annie brush her long hair, which is a golden color. Joanie knows that if she forgets to brush her hair, it will begin to get tangles in it. It will be difficult to brush then! Mom told her that brushing keeps her hair clean, because brushing takes out the dust. Her brother, Johnny, and her younger brother, Tommy, only need to use a comb to keep their hair looking nice.

One day, Joanie asked, "Mother, my friend Sally braids her hair. Can you show me how to braid my hair? Should I make two braids or one braid? One of the older girls at church is from Sweden, and she says lots of the girls there wear their braids on top of their heads! Mother, can you show me different ways to braid my hair?"

"Certainly, I will show you, Joanie! The important thing to remember is that you always want to look clean and neat. But it is fun to experiment with different ways to wear your hair!"

Johnny stopped at the door, combing his hair.

"Why does Johnny have that funny patch of hair sticking up on the top of his head?" Joanie asked her mother.

"Well, Joanie, Johnny has a cowlick! Those pieces of hair just don't want to stay down!"

"Mother," Johnny asked, "why is this piece of hair sticking up called a cowlick? Will I have this strange cowlick the rest of my life?"

"Johnny, I suggest you ask your Dad about that! I don't think anyone knows why we call that a cowlick, but your dad probably had a cowlick at your age! Put a little water on it, and see if it stays down!"

Health 3 for Young Catholics

Johnny reached for the water bottle and sprayed his hair. "I know that cowlick will not stay down for long, Mom!"

The next day, it was pouring rain. Johnny was running home from the baseball game, but his shoes were becoming more and more muddy. His socks felt soggy! Johnny asked his guardian angel to help him to get home safely and to help him not to get a cold, because he was so wet!

As he approached the back door, Johnny knew Mother would not like to see his muddy shoes. So he pushed open the door as quickly and as quietly as he could!

"Is that you, Johnny?" his mother called from inside the house.

"Yes, Mother!"

"You know what to do with your muddy shoes, Johnny!"

"Yes, Mother!"

Johnny knew the rules. He turned around and took off his muddy sneakers, and tried to wipe them off on the mat just outside the door. But they were still muddy. Mother had a box right inside the door for muddy shoes to dry out, so Johnny opened the door and threw his shoes in the box.

Johnny thought about his Sunday shoes. He saves his black shoes for Sunday Mass. He sometimes serves at the 8 o'clock Mass. Dad always checks his black shoes on Saturday night to make sure they are clean and highly polished.

Father Burns told Johnny it is a great honor to be an altar boy. Johnny knows that when he is on the altar, the people are looking at him, and they expect him to be clean and neat.

"Johnny," his mother called again, "are you coming? Did you put your shoes in the drying-out box?"

"Yes, Mother, I'm coming."

Johnny walked into the dining room and saw his mother helping Joanie with her math.

"Are you dried out yet, Johnny? Do you think you should go upstairs and put on dry clothes?"

"Yes, Mother, I'll go and do that."

Johnny went up the stairs to his room. He looked in his dresser for a dry short-sleeve shirt. Then he looked in his closet.

Health 3 for Young Catholics

He saw his white Sunday shirt with the tie around the top of the hanger. His trousers hung on a special hanger next to it. Dad told him he must hang up his Sunday clothes immediately when he takes them off, so that they won't be wrinkled when he needs them again for Mass.

Johnny thought about how every Sunday, Dad checks how he is dressed. Johnny puts on his white shirt, then Dad checks to make sure his shirt tails are tucked inside. His father has shown him that wearing a belt helps to keep the shirt neatly in place. Last Christmas, Dad gave him a new belt with a silver buckle. Johnny touched that shiny buckle, and was happy to be so well-dressed for serving on the altar.

Johnny looked at his beautiful blue tie. Dad always checks it to make sure it does not have spots. Dad told him not to eat anything when he is wearing his tie.

"If you are given something to eat after Mass by Father Burns or by someone in the parish, be sure to take off your tie and put it in your pocket," Dad would remind him.

Last week, Johnny asked Father Burns to say a special Mass for his family. He asked Father to keep it a secret.

Johnny knew that Dad was proud of him for being an altar boy. His Dad had been an altar boy when he was a boy. "When Tommy gets older," Johnny thought, "he could be an altar boy too!"

"I can show Tommy how to be a good altar boy," Johnny said to himself. "Tommy can be an altar boy for Father Lane," Johnny thought. "Father Lane likes to train the younger boys."

## Lesson Review

1. Why is it important to brush or comb your hair every day?

_____

Health 3 for Young Catholics

2. What does Johnny do if his shoes are muddy?

   _____

3. On what day should clothes look especially neat?

   _____

4. What does Johnny do with his tie before eating?

   _____

5. How does a belt help Johnny?

   _____

6. How do you know that Johnny cares about his younger brother?

   _____

   _____

## Activities

Some girls know how to braid their hair. Here is how to make a simple braid with yarn. You will need yarn, tape, and cardboard (or another firm surface):

1. Take three strands of yarn, each of the same length (about 12 inches).

2. Lay the pieces of yarn next to one another on the cardboard.

3. Firmly tape the tops of the yarn to the cardboard. Be sure it will not come off when tugged.

4. Take the strand on the right side and move it to the middle position.

5. Then take the strand on the left side and move it to the middle position.

6. Continue steps 4 and 5 until you have almost run out of yarn.

7. Tie the bottoms together with a pretty ribbon.

If you have a sister or mother with long hair, maybe she will let you practice braiding her hair! Then you can learn how to braid your own hair if it is long enough.

## Cowlick

Do you have a cowlick? Have you seen pictures of boys with a cowlick? Ask your Dad how to manage a cowlick!

## Did You Know?

The hair you see is not alive. Only the follicle or the root of the hair is living. The follicle pushes hair cells up through the skin. Because the hair is not alive, there is no feeling in your hair when you cut it. That is why it doesn't hurt to get a hair cut, but it does hurt to have your hair pulled! Ouch!

# Chapter 3. Cleanliness Is Next to Godliness

The Martins arrived at church just in time for a few quiet prayers before Mass started. Sometimes their father was able to come to daily Mass with them, since he worked nearby. He always came on Saturday morning.

Theresa always tried to be helpful with the little ones at Mass. Today, she helped by holding Baby Rosie. Sometimes Rosie wanted to crawl around on the floor or put her mouth on the back of the pew. Theresa kept her from doing these things. She knew that the church was a place where many people came. That means there would be a good chance of catching a cold, or some other sickness that someone might have, from touching the pew. If she allowed Rosie to put her mouth on the pew, the germs from someone's sickness would go right into her little sister's mouth. Theresa would feel terrible if Baby Rosie got sick!

Theresa would often pray to her patron saint, St. Therese, the Little Flower. She would ask St. Therese to help her take care of the younger children for her mom. She knew that St. Therese, when she was little, was taken care of by her older sisters, so St. Therese would know how important it is to take care of younger children. Theresa would often look at her holy card with a picture of St. Therese.

Theresa remembered when Tommy used to suck his thumb. He was always getting sick! Mother said it was because when he touched something, there was not always a chance to wash his hands in time. His thumb put the germs right into his little mouth! Theresa thought that the guardian angels of little children must work overtime trying to protect them from germs and sickness!

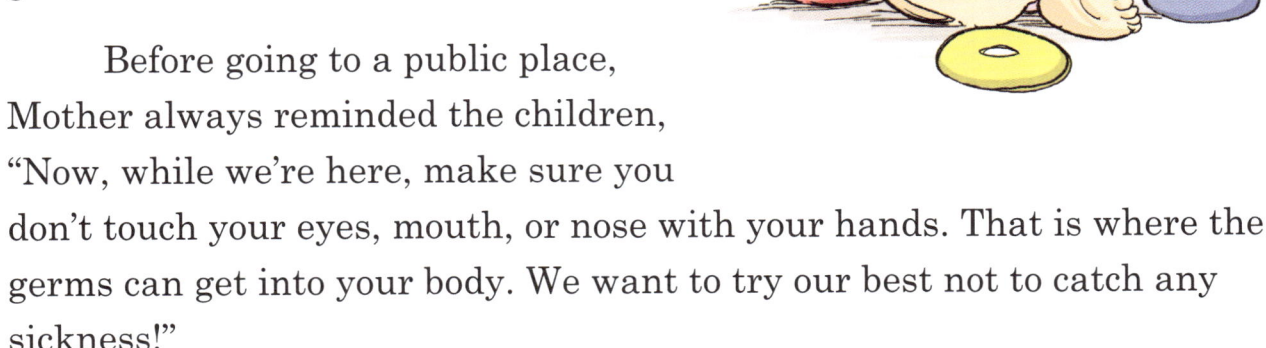

Before going to a public place, Mother always reminded the children, "Now, while we're here, make sure you don't touch your eyes, mouth, or nose with your hands. That is where the germs can get into your body. We want to try our best not to catch any sickness!"

It was sometimes easy to forget, but the children did try to keep their hands away from their eyes, mouth, and nose during Mass, or when they were at any public place. Mother always kept a bottle of hand sanitizer in the family's van. Even so, she reminded them to wash their hands as soon as they returned home.

When the Martin family arrived home from Mass that day, the children busily settled in.

"I want a snack!" begged Tommy.

"What do you say?" asked Mother.

"Please!" he answered.

"Okay, Tommy," Mother answered. "But have you washed your hands yet?"

"No, I need help!"

Health 3 for Young Catholics

"Joanie, will you help Tommy wash his hands, while I get everyone a little snack or a drink?" asked Mother.

"Yes, Mother!" Joanie responded cheerfully.

Joanie took Tommy to the bathroom and pulled the little stool out for him to stand on. She turned the water on to warm it up, like Mom said to do. Mom said to use as much warm water as possible to help kill the germs. Joanie then grabbed the soap bottle to squirt into his hands.

"Are you ready, Tommy? Put out your hands," Joanie said. Tommy put his hands out while Joanie squirted some soap onto them. "Now rub your hands together and make some bubbles!"

Tommy rubbed his hands.

"Look at all the bubbles!" cried Tommy.

"I see! That is what is making your hands clean. It's washing away all the bad germs that might make you sick! But you need to rub them long enough. Tommy, don't forget what Dad told you yesterday after you were playing with the dog next door!"

J.M.J.

"I don't remember what he said, Joanie!" screamed Tommy.

"Stop screaming, Tommy! Dad said you must wash under your nails, because you keep getting dirt under them!"

"How can I wash under my nails?" Tommy screamed.

"Hush, Tommy! Let me show you. Sometimes I scratch the soap bar to get the soap under my nails! Sometimes, I just scratch the soap suds from the palm of my other hand! If you see black under your nails, Tommy, you better scratch the soap bar!"

"Okay, but it is so slippery!"

"Well, let's sing the ABC's while you wash your hands," said Joanie.

"Mom said we should wash our hands for 20 seconds."

Joanie and Tommy started singing, but Joanie liked to quietly say the prayer to her guardian angel, which took just about that long to pray!

Tommy and Joanie sang together as he washed his hands.

That was fun!" said Tommy. "Now I want a snack! My stomach is gugling, like Dad says!"

"Not gugling, Silly, gurgling! Gurgling is what Dad says when he is hungry!"

"Well, mine is gugling!"

"Okay! Dry off your hands and go to the kitchen for your snack!"

The children liked to share their snacks and other food. Mom said that if they were with friends, they should be happy to share, but they must share carefully. Mom said the best way to share was to break the food and offer a piece. "Never allow another child to bite off a piece!"

Last week, when Johnny went to art class at the library, he broke off

Health 3 for Young Catholics

J.M.J.

half his sandwich and gave it to his friend Bobby. That way, Bobby would not get his germs!

"Germs are spread by eating something that has already had another person's mouth touch it," Mom would say. "And we cannot do that, even for each other in the family! Someone might be coming down with a cold or something else! Be careful, and don't share drinks from the same cup either!"

Mom was pretty strict, and would even send Tommy to his room if he drank out of someone's else's cup or ate food off of someone else's plate.

"It is not kind to anyone for you to get sick because you were careless, or to cause someone else to get sick because you let them eat or drink from your glass or plate! You can share your toys but not your germs!"

Mom said there are other things that carry germs and should not be shared. "Some items carry germs, just like hands do," she said. "Combs, hairbrushes, plates, cups and glasses, forks, spoons, napkins, and, of course, toothbrushes, cannot be shared," Mother would declare!

One time, after the family returned from the library, Mom talked to them about the library books.

"Children, unless books are new, they are dirty, because they have been held by many hands—especially children's books. Even the books we have here in the house are used or read by several of us," reminded Mother. "Some of the books you younger children are reading were read first by Theresa and Joanie. So, whenever you finish reading a used book, especially

20            Health 3 for Young Catholics

one from the library, wash your hands. It's also a good idea to clean your hands with sanitizer after touching a door knob or a light switch. They can carry the most germs of all, because everyone touches them! I know this seems strict, but in a big family, we need to do all we can to keep everyone from getting sick!"

Dad had a rule for the children about not using water fountains. "Never drink out of a water fountain unless you are desperate. Water fountains carry germs because some children accidentally put their mouth on the spigot where the water comes out! If you are desperate and need a drink, never touch the spigot; keep your mouth away from it!"

One time, when little Tommy needed a drink, his brother Johnny helped him use the water fountain. Johnny said, "I know you're very thirsty from playing outside. I will give you a plastic cup. But to be extra careful, to be extra safe, we'll let the water run for a little bit first."

Johnny ran the water for about 15 seconds, then he filled up a plastic cup with water and gave it to Tommy.

Sometimes Mom would bring water bottles in the car when the children were playing at the playground, so that they would not need to use the water fountain. "Even warm water from a bottle is better than getting sick," Mom would declare.

Dad had an important saying for the Martin children: "In a family, germs spread very easily! If we want to be good Catholics, we must not only take care of ourselves; we must also take care of others in the family by trying not to get sick and by not causing others to get sick!"

Dad put a sign up in red letters in the bathroom. It looked like this:

## Wash Your Hands:

- Before and after preparing food
- Before eating
- After reading a used book
- After using the bathroom
- After sneezing, coughing, or blowing your nose
- Before and after helping someone who is sick
- Before and after taking care of a cut
- Before touching a baby
- After changing a diaper
- After touching an animal
- After taking out the garbage

## Lesson Review

1. Why is it important not to touch your eyes, mouth, or nose when you are at church?

   _____

   _____

2. What can germs do to you?

   _____

3. What should you do after being in a public place?

   _____

4. Name something that should not be shared.

   _____

5. Name a time when you should wash your hands.

   _____

## Activities

Have you ever used a public restroom? You will see a sign near the sink, listing the steps for washing your hands. With your parents' permission, make a sign for the sinks in your house. Below is a list that you may copy. You may add pictures if you'd like.

1. Wet your hands under warm running water.

2. Add soap to your hands.

3. Lather and scrub your hands for 20 seconds.

4. Rinse your hands under warm running water.

5. Turn off the water.

6. Dry your hands.

**"And I will pour upon you clean water, and you shall be cleansed…."
(Ezekiel 36:25)**

## Did You Know?

If we eat healthy food and get plenty of sleep, our bodies will be strong, and they will be able to fight off bad germs. Have you noticed that after a birthday party or holiday, you sometimes get sick? That is because eating too much sugar makes your body weak. If you don't overdo it with sweets, your body will be strong enough to fight off many of the bad germs that come your way!
Here is a poem for you!

**Too Much Sugar!**

Too much sugar!
Too much sugar!
What a toothache!
How I'm sick from
Too much sugar.

24

Health 3 for Young Catholics

# Chapter 4. Care of Teeth and Eyes

"Hey, Mom! I think Rosie is getting another tooth!" Johnny exclaimed.

The Martin family was sitting in the living room one Sunday afternoon. Dad was doing a crossword puzzle. Mom was in the kitchen.

"That makes sense," Mother answered from the kitchen. "Rosie has been a little bit grumpy lately. I don't blame her! It must hurt for that sharp little tooth to pop through her baby gums. Hopefully, it will feel better, now that we can see it coming in."

"I remember when my six-year molars came in," said Joanie. "It was sore in the back of my mouth for a couple of weeks. I know how Rosie must feel!"

"Yes," said Dad, as he looked up from his crossword puzzle. "It can be a bit sore when a tooth comes in, even for older people. Those six-year molars are different, however, from your other teeth. The teeth that came in when you were a baby are called primary teeth. They are the ones that wiggle and fall out."

"I remember when my baby teeth fell out!" proclaimed Johnny. "I remember they hurt for a few days!"

"Baby teeth hurt babies when they come in, like Rosie's. And baby teeth hurt when they come out! They usually start coming out when children are about six years old."

"I think I still have some little teeth, Dad!"

"That could be, Johnny. Let me take a look!"

Health 3 for Young Catholics

"Johnny, you are right! You still have a few small teeth back there! By the time you are twelve, you should have all your adult teeth (except your wisdom teeth, which come in much later). We call the second set, your adult teeth, permanent teeth. That's because you will hopefully have them the rest of your life. It's very important to take good care of all your teeth, but especially the permanent teeth."

"Which are the permanent teeth, Dad?" asked Johnny.

"Johnny, you should have about twenty-four teeth right now, but after your 12-year molars come in, and then later your wisdom teeth, you'll have as many as thirty-two teeth!"

"Dad, how can thirty-two teeth fit in my mouth?" Johnny asked.

"Well, as your body grows, Johnny, your mouth grows and makes room for more teeth!"

"I'm going to count them," said Johnny. "I am going to look in the bathroom mirror!"

Johnny walked out of the room. He came back about 15 minutes later.

"Well, Johnny, it took you a long time to count twenty-four teeth!"

"Well, I did count twenty-four teeth. I do have twenty-four in my mouth! Joanie, do you want to see them?"

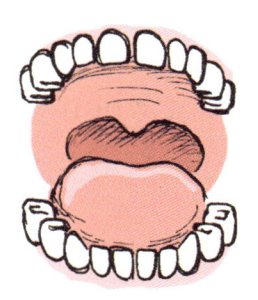

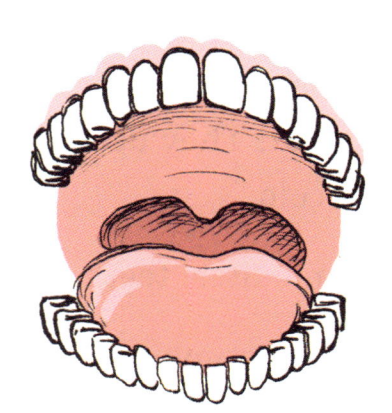

Johnny suddenly leaned over the chair where his sister was sitting. "See my twenty-four teeth?"

J.M.J.

"Eeew! That's awful! Daaaad, Johnny's teeth are GREEEEEN!"

"See my teeth, Annie! Don't you like my beautiful green teeth!"

"Oh! They are ugly!" cried Annie, giggling.

"What did you do, Johnny?" asked Joanie. "It looks like you colored them green with something!"

"I used Mom's food coloring!"

"Well, hopefully, you'll take care of your teeth, and they won't look even a little like that!" said Dad. "Since everyone is so interested in teeth, maybe this is a good time to review how to take care of your teeth. Since you are having so much fun, Johnny, you can be the clown to show everyone else how to brush your teeth properly!"

Dad took Joanie, Johnny, Annie, and even three-year old Tommy over to the bathroom.

"Johnny, take out your toothbrush and your toothpaste."

"Okay, kids. Here are a few rules! Johnny, you follow the rules as I say them!"

J.M.J.

"First, use a soft toothbrush. Your teeth are still soft. Feel the brush with your fingers."

"It feels only a little soft, Dad!" exclaimed Johnny.

"Okay, Johnny! Now wet your brush under the water. Then put a finger-nail-size bit of toothpaste on your brush. That's right, Johnny! Now let's see how you brush your teeth. First brush the outside of the top teeth, then brush the outside of the bottom teeth. You are doing fine, Johnny! Now brush at an angle, so that you brush your gums as well. Your gums need to be lightly brushed to keep them free of food pieces. Okay, now brush the inside of the top teeth, then the inside of the bottom teeth. That looks good, Johnny. Now, finally, brush the tops of the teeth."

"Be sure to spit into the sink whenever your mouth gets too full of water or toothpaste," reminded Dad. "Of course, spit out the water and paste when you are finished. Try not to swallow the toothpaste. Finally, rinse out your mouth with water, and make sure the sink is clean."

"That's fun, Dad. Let's practice it again," declared Annie.

"Never mind, Annie. You are only five, and you don't need a lot of practice! But Joanie, now that you are twelve, you should be using floss."

" Mother," Dad called out to Mom, who was in the kitchen, "do you have some floss in the downstairs bathroom?"

"It's on the top shelf," Mom said from the kitchen.

"What is floss, Dad," asked three-year-old Tommy.

Dad took out the little white floss box from the shelf in the bathroom cabinet.

"Well, Tommy, floss is a special, very thin string used for cleaning between the teeth. It is mainly for older children and adults. It should be done at bedtime, so that pieces of food do not remain between the teeth during the night. Flossing helps get out any extra pieces of food that might get stuck between the teeth, that the brush cannot reach. If the food stays there too long, it will begin to cause decay in the teeth."

"I have seen Theresa floss her teeth," said Joanie. "Are John and I old enough to start flossing."

"Well, I think you are both old enough, but parents must decide when to have their children start flossing, Joanie. The dentist often suggests an age. Some dentists think children should start flossing their teeth at about six years old. Here, Johnny, you watch how I floss. Then you try it."

After Dad showed him, Johnny started flossing between his teeth. He was especially careful to floss the teeth that were close together. He needed to catch any bits of food that were more likely to get stuck and cause decay.

"Great job, Johnny!" Dad said. "Now remember to brush every evening at bedtime, and even after eating any sweets, if you can—or after eating any food, like nuts, that might get stuck between your teeth. Floss every day before you go to bed. Hopefully, no one in the family will get any cavities!"

"Another thing about having good teeth is that we can enjoy eating good food because we can chew our meat, eat fruit and vegetables, and have happy meals, together! Right Mother?" asked Father.

"You are right about that!" declared Mother.

"Dad, my friend Christine has braces on her teeth. Do they keep her from getting cavities," asked Joanie.

"No, they aren't for that, Joanie," explained Dad. "Sometimes when the permanent teeth grow in, they do not come in as straight as they should. The braces are put on the teeth by a special kind of dentist called an orthodontist. The braces have little wires that gently pull the teeth back into place over a few years, so that they become nice and straight. Probably in two years, you'll see Christine's teeth all straightened out!"

"Wow! They look nice on her. She even has colored braces! I wonder if I'll ever need braces."

"I certainly hope not, Joanie. They are very expensive."

"Well," said Joanie, "I noticed that Christine has purple-colored braces. She said they come in different colors. If I ever need braces, I'll get pink ones!"

Mother walked in to hear Joanie.

"Joanie," said Mother, "you don't want braces, if at all possible. They are very uncomfortable. Anyone with braces will tell you that. If you ever have a problem with your teeth, ask St. Apollonia to help. She is the patroness of dentists and for people who suffer with toothaches."

"I never heard of St. Apollonia, Mother!" exclaimed Joanie.

"A long time ago, in Egypt," began Mother, "when many people did not believe in the One True God, the bad pagan government commanded Apollonia to give up her Catholic Faith. She would not. The Egyptian ruler ordered Apollonia to change her mind; if not, she would be punished, he said. God's grace kept Apollonia brave, and she did not give up her Faith. As her punishment, the cruel ruler ordered that all her teeth be removed! Then, poor Apollonia was killed. Because Apollonia was a martyr, choosing to die rather than give up her Faith, the Catholic Church proclaims that she is now a saint in Heaven. We must pray to St. Apollonia to help us take care of our teeth, and that none of us have problems with our teeth!"

"I'll say Amen to that!" declared Dad.

Theresa came downstairs and saw Dad and the children. "I heard you talk about braces, Dad," said Theresa. "But I was wondering if some of us will need to wear glasses like you sometimes do when you read the newspaper."

J.M.J.

"Well, that is likely, Theresa, I am sorry to say. Now that you are fourteen, we really need to have your eyes checked. You have not complained, but sometimes people need glasses, and they don't realize it. They don't realize that with eyeglasses, they could see better!"

"I don't think I have a problem, but I would like to go to the eye doctor and find out if I can see better!" exclaimed Theresa.

"We will do that, Theresa," responded Father. "The eyes are made of muscles, and, as we grow older, the muscles tend to become weaker. In addition, since many people are now spending a great deal of time on the computer, looking at the computer screen for a long time, more and more people are likely to need to wear glasses. In fact, now doctors are providing glasses specifically for working on the computer!"

"Thanks, Dad! By the way, is there a patron saint for good vision?"

"Yes, Theresa. St. Lucy is the patron saint for good eyesight," said Dad. "We can pray to her to help us have good eyesight, and also to protect us from eye diseases, especially infections of the eye. It is not uncommon for young children to get eye infections if they wipe their eyes with dirty fingers!"

"And I think we should take some of the other children to the eye doctor, Father," Mother said from the kitchen. "We should check out the other children to make sure we know whether or not they need glasses!"

"I will try to make an appointment tomorrow with Dr. Miller!" Father answered.

"Did I hear someone talk about going to the eye doctor?" asked Joanie as she walked in the room.

"Yes, Joanie!"

"I was wondering, Dad, why you wear eyeglasses when you read the newspaper, but Mom wears glasses when she drives!"

"That is because we have two different reasons for wearing glasses, Joanie. I need to wear glasses when I read. In fact, I call them my reading glasses. I am farsighted. I cannot read things that are close, but I have good eyesight for things that are far, so I don't need glasses to drive," explained Dad.

"And, Joanie," replied Mom, "I am nearsighted. I can see things that are near better than I can see things that are at a distance. So I need to put on my glasses when I drive."

"Well, Children, maybe we all need to see the eye doctor and check up on our vision," Dad said. "I may need stronger glasses, anyway—especially since I am reading so many bedtime stories these days!"

## Lesson Review

1. What is your first set of teeth called?

2. What is your second set of teeth called?

   _____

3. How many teeth does an adult have?

   _____

4. When is the most important time of the day to brush your teeth?

   _____

5. Who is the patron saint of people with toothaches?

   _____

6. How do children get eye infections?

   _____

7. Who is the patron saint of those with eye problems?

   _____

## Activities

To do a good job brushing your teeth, you should take about one minute. Try to learn how long one minute is by singing a song you know, like Happy Birthday. Watch the clock and see how many times you need to sing the song for one minute. Try it with a few different songs or prayers that you know well. Choose the one you'd like to use. Then, when you brush, you'll be able to sing the song in your head to make sure you're brushing for long enough!

   A project that some children and moms find interesting is making their own toothpaste: Here is what you will need:

- 4 teaspoons of baking soda
- 1 teaspoon of salt
- 1 teaspoon of flavoring (peppermint, vanilla, or almond extract)
- An airtight container

Mix all the ingredients together. Keep the mixture sealed in the airtight container until it's time to use it. You may want to keep a small plastic spoon handy to help spread it onto your toothbrush when it is time to brush.

## Did You Know?

The toothbrush was invented more than 500 years ago by the Chinese. However, it took a long time for toothpaste to be invented. Toothpaste has been around for only about 100 years. For the many, many years before that, people tried other "cleaners" on their teeth: ground-up chalk, lemon juice, ashes, or tobacco and honey mixed together. You can see that people were desperate to keep their teeth clean, and most people eventually lost almost all their teeth. We are certainly fortunate to have peppermint-flavored toothpaste that is easy to find at the nearest grocery store!

Eyeglasses were not invented until sometime in the 1200s, when many inventions and scientific discoveries were being made in Europe. It is believed that an Italian monk was responsible for the first pair of what we would consider eyeglasses. His name was Alessandro della Spina. Apparently, the frames were made of metal, and the lenses were made of quartz. Quartz is a hard mineral that looks like glass.

Those of us who wear glasses should thank God for helping Alessandro, and all those who came after him, who worked on making better glasses, so that we can see all the beautiful things God has made in the world! Just think about all the beautiful things you can see, such as the sunrise and the sunset, flowers, the rainbow, and the stars. What are some of your favorite things to see?

# Chapter 5. Healthy Eating: Nutrition

Mrs. Martin was sitting in the warm kitchen, thinking about what she would buy for the week's meals.

"Mom," Johnny began, "may I have a second helping of your delicious apple pie? After all, apples are healthy, aren't they?"

Mother smiled and then answered, "Yes, Johnny, I will give you a second piece of pie. Apples are good for you, Johnny, but in the pie, the apples are mixed with sugar. That's what makes it such a delicious treat! But we all need to eat more fruit without sugar! God has made fruit naturally sweet. The kind of sweetness in fruit is healthier than the sugar in the pie!"

Mother cut another piece of pie for Johnny, who immediately sat down to eat it.

"Johnny, we need to think about eating enough vegetables, too. I am making my shopping list, and each week I include vegetables and fruit."

"When you make the salad for dinner, Mom, I notice that you put apples in the middle of the vegetables!"

"That is my way, Johnny, of encouraging you to eat the healthy fruit along with the healthy vegetables. Vegetables give our bodies the vitamins and minerals they need."

"Will we be able to eat whatever we want in Heaven, Mother?" asked Johnny.

"The Bible calls Heaven a great wedding feast, so I know we will all be very happy with the food there!" Mother answered.

J.M.J.

Dad came into the kitchen. "Well, it is starting to snow outside! It is going to be a wintry day. Mother, maybe we should put off the shopping trip until it stops snowing!"

"I was just thinking about which vegetables and fruits I would purchase this morning," declared Mother.

"Let's gather the children together," suggested Father, "and talk about fruits and vegetables, which are important in our diet! Perhaps this afternoon, the weather will be better, and you can purchase the foods they like, as well as the foods they need for good nutrition!"

"That sounds like a great idea! Johnny, why don't you go and tell the others to come here in the kitchen, and we can talk about nutrition," said Mother, "and the foods each of us likes to eat!"

In a few minutes, the children started entering the kitchen.

Health 3 for Young Catholics

"Hey, Children!" Father began. "I'd like us to spend some time talking about good nutrition. Here is my idea: let's have each of you start talking about your favorite fruits and vegetables, and what Mom can purchase at the store today."

"Okay, Dad," Fourteen-year old Therese said.

"Sounds like fun, Dad," twelve-year old Joanie declared.

"Well, I know what I like!" ten-year old Johnny stated with vigor.

"Can I ask for strawberries, Dad?" asked five-year old Annie.

"Mommy, can I have some grapes?" asked three-year old Tommy.

J.M.J.

"Well," responded Mother, "It sounds like everyone wants to get involved. Little Rose, since she is only eight months old, can eat some fruits, but we need to mash them up so that she can eat them."

"Okay, Children," declared Dad. "I will start by mentioning foods in each food group, and you each can pick the ones you like best. Okay?"

"That's a great idea, Father!" Mother joined in.

"Okay, Children! Let's start! There are four main food groups. Does anyone know what they are?"

"Sure, Dad, I already studied that," said Theresa. "All healthy foods belong in the milk group, the meat group, the fruit and vegetable group, or the grain group."

"That's great, Theresa," declared Father. "Of course, some popular foods, such as candy, belong to a sweets group, and some other popular snacks, such as potato chips, belong to another group called fats. But we won't talk about those right now. We will talk about the four main healthy groups, and choose foods we like from the four groups: milk, meat, grains, and fruits and vegetables."

"Theresa, since you are the oldest, why don't we start with you. Will you take the grains group?" asked Dad. "What foods are in the grains group, and which of those do you like best?"

"Okay, Dad. I know that different breads and cereals, like oatmeal, as well crackers, rice, and pasta, are in the grains category. Of course, my favorites are pasta and pizza! Can we have pizza for dinner tonight, Mom?"

Health 3 for Young Catholics

"Okay, that's great, Theresa! You know your grains! Of course, as for dinner tonight, your mom and I will need to talk about that! One thing we must remember, however, is that there are healthy breads and healthy cereals. We want to make sure we avoid having too much white bread or white rice, because they turn into sugar in our bodies. Having too much white bread or white rice can be like eating too much junk food. So, Mother never buys white bread!"

"I know too many children who eat only white bread," said Mother. "It is not bad for you every now and then, but eating healthy grain bread is much better for staying in good health."

"Okay, Joanie, you are next," declared Father. "Since you are twelve, I know you can tell us about the meat group!"

"Well, I know about beef because I like hamburgers! And I like the outside piece when Mom makes roast beef for dinner! Yum, yum! And I know that grandpa likes a pork roast! Sometimes he even brings one over on Sunday, and he says he likes to cook it 'just right.' And then there is chicken, which I know the little children like!"

"I like chicken legs!" little Annie chimed in.

"One thing I don't understand, though," said Joanie, 'is that fish is in the same category as meat! I guess it has to do with the same kind of vitamins."

"Well," said Dad, "Fish is very high in protein, like meat. In fact, per ounce, fish has even more protein than meat! Having tuna fish patties or a tuna casserole, like your mom makes on Fridays, really gives us great nutrition!"

"Well," declared Joanie, "that must be the reason why eggs, beans, and nuts are included in the meat group. They are so high in the same kind of protein!"

"You are correct about that, Joanie," Mother said. "Which of those do you like best?"

"Well, I do like peanuts, but really, scrambled eggs are my favorite for a nonmeat in the meat group. Of course, I like to eat them with real meat, like bacon or sausage!" laughed Joanie.

"Well, let's remember why foods from the meat group are important," said Mother. "These foods help keep our hair, skin, nails, muscles, blood, and inner organs of our body healthy. These foods also give us the protein and iron that our bodies need for energy."

"Well, Johnny and Tommy don't need to eat any more meat than they are having already! They seem to have an extra portion of energy!" declared Theresa.

"Okay, okay!" said Dad. "Now let's ask Johnny. Son, what do you like in the fruits and vegetables group?"

"Well, Dad, I like lots of fruits but not too many vegetables!"

Health 3 for Young Catholics

"I could have guessed that," Dad declared, "from your plate at the end of a meal! Well, tell us your favorite fruits, Johnny!"

"I like bananas; they are my favorites!"

"No wonder he acts like a monkey!" exclaimed Joanie.

"Well, at least I am getting plenty of exercise!" yelled Johnny!

"Okay, okay! Johnny, what else do you like?" asked Dad.

"Well, I like lots of fruits, especially strawberries on top of cake and covered with whipped cream! And I like grapes to eat when I am in my tree house! And I like peaches, and oranges when they don't have too many seeds! And I like apples when they are not too hard," declared Johnny.

"But," continued Johnny, " I really don't care for watermelon; it is too messy! It drips all over my shirt! And I don't like lemons, except in lemonade! And I don't like cherries and plums, because I need to eat around the pits! I don't like pineapples or pears. I don't like blueberries unless Mom makes a blueberry pie with ice cream on top! Yum! Yum!"

"Okay, Johnny, I get the picture," exclaimed Dad. "I know you don't care for vegetables in general. Mother, why don't you tell us the vegetables you like?"

"Okay!" Mother agreed. "Well, when I was younger, there were not very many vegetables I liked, but now I like more vegetables. I try to buy the vegetables that some of you like, and some that maybe you will like eventually."

"Okay, Mother!" said Theresa. "Which do you like?"

J.M.J.

"My favorites are peas, carrots, corn, potatoes, sweet potatoes, tomatoes, beans, broccoli, and lettuce," Mother declared.

"Well," said Johnny, "I sure don't like spinach!"

"Don't forget Popeye, Johnny! He got his strength from spinach!" answered Dad.

"Okay, Dad!" responded Johnny.

"Just remember, everybody," Dad started. "Vegetables and fruits give our bodies the vitamins and minerals they need. Our eyes need Vitamin A from carrots. Vitamin C from oranges helps heal cuts and wounds. Remember that, Johnny!"

Dad continued. "Fruits and vegetables help our bodies fight off illnesses. We need to eat vegetables every day to keep healthy and not get sick. If someone in our family gets the flu or some other contagious disease, it is likely that everyone in the family will get it! So we all need to think as a family team, to keep ourselves healthy so that we can keep the entire family healthy. Keep in mind that the dark green vegetables and the brightly colored vegetables have the most vitamins and minerals."

"Okay, Annie! We are ready for you to tell us about the milk group," said Dad. "I know this is one of your favorite groups, because I know you like ice cream!"

"Yes, Daddy! Can Mom buy some chocolate ice cream today?"

"We will see, Annie. But, right now, tell us about your favorite food in the milk group."

"Well, ice cream is my favorite! I don't understand why I can't have ice cream instead of milk in my cereal!"

"Annie," began Theresa, "we all know you like sweet ice cream, but if you had as much ice cream as you need milk at every meal, you would soon get sick, not to mention fat!" declared Theresa, rather vociferously!

"Okay, okay! Sometimes I like just plain milk! And I like cheese, especially when Mom makes a melted cheese sandwich! I like to put lots of butter on it! Or ice cream on top! Ha! Ha! And, one time, we had an all-cheese pizza; I like that kind the best. And I like whipped cream when Mom whips up the cream and let's me taste it while she is making it! Yum, yum! I like whipped cream on cookies and even on birthday cakes! And when Mom gave me yogurt with strawberries, I stirred in whipped cream! I really liked that! Mom, can you buy more whipped cream so that I can help you whip it?"

"Okay, Annie! Good for you!" exclaimed Dad. "You really know your foods in the milk group! And, just so you know, I like cream in my coffee! Foods in the milk group are great because they help our teeth and bones grow strong. Annie, you still have baby teeth, so you need foods in the milk group to keep your teeth healthy, and to keep your big teeth healthy, too! Besides helping our teeth, foods in the milk group help our muscles and our hearts work better!"

"Well, that explains it, Dad! Because she is eating so much ice cream and whipped cream, it is affecting her heart. That is why she LOVES ice cream with all her heart!" declared Theresa.

"Annie is in LOVE with ice cream!" shouted Johnny. Everyone laughed, including Annie!

"Daddy," Tommy chimed in, "I like milk! But I like chocolate milk a little better than plain milk."

J.M.J.

"And I know what Baby Rosie, likes, Dad," offered Theresa. "She LOVES chocolate custard pudding! She especially likes it all over her face!"

"Good for all you children! You really know the foods in the food groups! There are a few other things I need to remind you about," said Dad. "Sweets are not good for our bodies. Foods such as cakes, pies, doughnuts, chips, and sugary cereals do not help our bodies."

"In fact, "continued Father, "we should limit the amounts of unhealthy snacks we eat. Sugary foods can cause tooth decay, because they make bacteria grow on our teeth. Snacking with these foods in between meals not only causes cavities to form; it also makes the stomach work too hard trying to get the good things out of the food to help your body. Unhealthy snacks can cause us to gain unwanted weight. Unhealthy snacks make it easier to get sick too. Our bodies do not have as much ability to fight off germs if we eat too much sugary foods and not enough healthy foods!"

"Foods considered 'fats' can be tricky," explained Father. "There are many fats that are not good for you, such as fat on meat, and that can be harmful to the body. Some fats, however, are very good for you, such as good butter and healthy oils, like olive oil, which helps your brain to work its best."

"Wow, Dad! Maybe I need some olive oil to help me with my algebra! Can you get some olives, Mom?" asked Theresa.

"Well, Theresa," explained Dad, "The best foods that contains olive oil are salad dressings. Let's see what Mom can do to find salad dressings

Health 3 for Young Catholics

with olive oil. Eating a good salad with olive oil could very well improve your algebra grades!"

"Thanks, Father, for helping us all to remember the importance of eating nutritious foods!" exclaimed Mother. "Now let's see how eating nutritious foods can improve all your test grades! Right, Father?"

"Sounds good to me," Father declared. "Healthy bodies make healthy brains, which make healthy grades!"

## Lesson Review

1. Are all foods healthy for you?

   _____

2. Which group is helpful for strong bones?

   _____

3. Name three foods from the meat group.

   _____

   _____

4. What kinds of vegetables have the most vitamins and minerals?

   _____

5. What is one reason not to have too many unhealthy snacks?

   _____

   _____

6. Name one food in each food group that you like.

   _____

   _____

   _____

   _____

## Activities

Keep a food diary. Write down the foods you eat every day for one week. At the end of the week, look at all you have eaten. Use different colors of crayons or markers to mark the foods that go together. Use one color for the milk group, another for the meat group, and so on. At the end of the week, look at what you wrote down. Think about whether there is a group that you need to eat more often. Did you have too many unhealthy snacks?

## Did You Know?

Have you ever felt a burst of energy after having sweets? Then, soon after, did you feel very sluggish? This comes from there being too much sugar in your blood at once, from the sweet treat. Protein in foods such as meat, eggs, and nuts, helps the sugars in your body to stay balanced. If you have a treat, try to have some kind of protein with it, and you might just be able to feel more energetic!

J.M.J.

# Chapter 6. Exercise and Respect

"Let's go!" Johnny yelled excitedly. "It's game day, and I want to get to the playground early!"

Johnny was running to the door, basketball in hand, as though the nearest basket were only a few feet in front of him!

"All right, Johnny! I know everyone is excited to go," explained Mother, "but I need to make sure that the little ones, Annie and Tommy, have finished eating, used the bathroom, and cleaned up. Also, I need to dress Baby Rosie!"

"I am so glad the other homeschooling families like to have a play day," declared Theresa. "I guess at fourteen, I don't like to run around quite as much, but I think Johnny and Tommy especially need all the running-around time they can get, Mom!"

"Yes, Theresa, you are right about that! But you need plenty of exercise, too. We all do! Would you please go out to the car and make sure the children have their seat belts on?" asked Mom.

Tommy came running into the kitchen. "I love game day!" he exclaimed.

"Me, too!" chimed in Annie.

"And I do too," said Mother.

"Really?" asked Joanie? "But you don't get a chance to play, Mom!"

"Well, I do get a bit of exercise chasing Tommy around! But I like game day for a different reason. I like to know that you are all getting the exercise you need," answered Mother.

"Come on, Children, let's all get in the van!"

Once in the van, the children all started talking at once.

"I know that I feel better when I exercise, but I don't know why!" exclaimed twelve-year old Joanie.

"The main reason you feel good when you exercise is that it gives you energy," explained Mom.

"When you do exercises," Mom continued, "like running, jumping, and biking, you breathe quite hard, don't you? That means you are getting more oxygen into your lungs. The oxygen goes from your lungs to your heart. Your heart is an important muscle, and it needs oxygen to be stronger. When your heart is stronger, you have more energy."

"Sometimes I run so much that I can barely catch my breath! I must be getting a lot of oxygen!" Johnny said with excitement.

"Actually, that is a little too much if you are having trouble breathing, Johnny! You shouldn't overdo it, because overdoing it is not good for your body. If you exercise often enough, without pushing yourself too hard, your heart will get stronger and stronger. Then you'll be able to do a little more each time," explained Mother.

"Is that why we take breaks on game day?" said Joanie.

"Yes, it is, Joanie. Sometimes boys and girls your age tend to overdo it when they exercise, which is not good, especially if they are not exercising every day. The parents in charge of the games don't want you to hurt yourselves. Taking a break also gives you a chance to have a drink of water. Your body uses a lot of water when you are exercising, so it is important to drink more water. It is even more important on a hot day, since you are sweating more and losing water from your body."

"What about the other exercises we do, Mother?" asked Theresa. "I know ballet is exercise, but most of the time, I don't breathe as hard as when I am running."

"During your slower exercises in ballet, you are working some different muscles," explained Mom. "You are stretching those muscles and making them more flexible. It is good for your muscles to be flexible or to be able to bend and stretch even more. You also are making your muscles stronger in your legs, arms, feet, and even your belly."

"We always warm up at ballet, and on game day too. If anyone comes to ballet late, without the warm-up, my teacher has her sit through the whole class!" said Theresa.

"Yes, that is because warming up is so important. When you do slower exercises and stretching before your more active exercises, it gets your muscles ready slowly. If you start exercising too hard without warming up, you can hurt yourself, and perhaps pull a muscle. If that happens, you might not be able to dance for several weeks."

"I love game day, but sometimes some children get upset when they lose a game," remarked Joanie.

"Well, that's something they need to work on," said Mother. "It can be very hard to lose. All the children need to remember that no one will win every time. But there always will be another chance to play. Whether you win or lose, you should treat others the way you would like to be treated, as our catechism teaches. If you win, don't brag or tease the other team. If you lose, it's good to say "Congratulations" to the other team. Tell them they did a good job or that it was a good game. That's what you would want to hear, isn't it? This is part of what is called 'good sportsmanship.'"

"I've heard that before," said Joanie. "I think it also means playing fair, doesn't it?"

"That's right," said Mother. "Good sportsmanship really means having good manners in your games. That means playing fair and being nice to the other team, whether you win or lose."

Health 3 for Young Catholics

"We're here!" yelled Johnny. The children took off their seat belts, jumped out of the car, and then helped carry things to the picnic area. Then they hurried over to their group. They were ready for an afternoon of fun and exercise.

After dinner that evening, Dad talked to the children about proper exercise and the games they played.

"What are some of the games you like to play at the playground?"

"Well," said fourteen-year-old Theresa, "my favorite game at the playground is badminton, but I also like to play basketball! They have very nice courts there!"

"I like riding my bike on the bike trails in the park area around the playground," declared Joanie. "My friends and I like to watch the little animals scurrying about, along the bike trails."

"Dad," proclaimed Johnny, "I like to play games with the other boys. We play baseball and basketball. I get really sweaty playing basketball, but I like baseball when I can hit the ball! I also like climbing on the jungle gym!"

"Annie, you are only five, but what games do you play at the playground?" asked Father.

"I like to jump rope with the other girls. I like to play tag. Sometimes we play hide and seek. Sometimes we play hopscotch!" explained Annie.

"Mother, what do you do with little Tommy at the playground?"

"Oh, Tommy loves to play Simon Says with the other little ones. Moms take turns being Simon. We do things they need to imitate, such as jumping in different ways and in different directions. We do hopping and skipping and crawling and running. Sometimes we run around trees or bushes. All the time, the little ones follow and imitate!"

"Children," Dad began, "physical exercise is important for all your life. If you want your body to be healthy, you must exercise to some extent every day. When you exercise, you will feel refreshed, and your muscles won't get sluggish. In fact, it might sound strange, but with exercise, even your brain won't get sluggish! If you want a good healthy life, for your body and your brain, exercise every day."

"Sometimes we can't go to the playground, Dad," said Johnny. "What do we do then?"

"Help around the yard," explained Dad. "Just raking and cleaning up the yard gives you plenty of exercise and the fresh air you need for healthy lungs!"

"What if it is raining or snowing! What should we do then, Dad?"

"I can keep you busy with exercise," Mom jumped in. "There is always plenty of work right in the house, such as taking the dirty laundry downstairs, and taking the clothes back upstairs after they are cleaned!"

"Sometimes, in the winter, we have family projects!" said Dad. "Bad weather days are good for moving things upstairs or downstairs. Such days also give us a chance to move furniture from one bedroom to another when someone in the family wants a different bedroom."

Dad continued, "We might have a carpentry project! Think about how many bookcases we have had to build for your school supplies! And remember the winter we built that new kitchen floor cabinet for Mother? And remember the time we built shelves in the garage to hold my tools? Bad weather days are good for catching up with building projects!"

"As the oldest child in this family," Theresa explained, "I get a lot of exercise doing things in this house! I would like to suggest that some of the other children help me more, just so that they can get more healthy exercise, of course!"

"Theresa, you make a good point!" exclaimed Dad. "While we all have duties around the house, inside and out, maybe we need to take a new look and make sure we all get the healthy exercise we need! Right, Children?"

"Right Dad," everyone answered somewhat lightly.

"I can't hear you!" responded Dad.

"Yes, Dad!" everyone shouted at once.

"Okay! Let's all go outside! We have some exercise to do!"

Dad took the children outside, where everyone was given a yard job! He made each child a part of a "team" for their jobs. Dad was even heard by some children to be singing, "This is the way we work today, work today, work today. This is the way we work today, to keep our bodies healthy!"

After dinner that evening, while the children ate their apple pie, Dad said he wanted to read them a list he had made.

"Here are some additional things to remember," Dad said, and he read the list out loud to the children. When he finished reading it, he posted this note on the refrigerator so that all the children could see it:

> **Daily exercise helps us to have strong muscles and bones.**
>
> **Daily exercise helps us to have a proper weight for our age.**
>
> **Daily exercise helps us to sleep better at night.**
>
> **Daily exercise helps our brains to work better and not feel sluggish.**
>
> **Daily exercise makes us feel happy.**
>
> **Daily exercise gives us more energy!**

"Wow, Dad!" exclaimed Johnny, "I did not know exercise could do so much!"

Health 3 for Young Catholics

"Yes, Johnny," Dad continued, "and most doctors believe a child your age should do some kind of exercise for at least an hour every day. If necessary, this can be spread out through the day. If you are chasing Bruno around the yard, that is pretty good exercise! Daily exercise is much easier than you may think. Many times, when you are playing, you are already exercising!"

"Father, you are certainly good with helping the children to be healthy," exclaimed Mother. "Right now, though, let's eat this delicious apple pie that Theresa helped me make! And we can thank Johnny who got his exercise picking the apples!"

"Do you all want me to tell you the story about Johnny Appleseed and how he got his exercise?" asked Father.

"No!" all the children responded heartily.

## Respect for Mom and Dad

"Dad, tomorrow is Mom's birthday and we are trying to make gifts for her!" declared Theresa.

"Mom will be pleased with any gifts made by you children," stated Dad.

"All week, we have been planning!"

"Yes, Theresa, I know that Johnny is in the garage now, and I need to go see how he is doing. He is making a jewelry box for Mother," explained Father. "Mother is at the supermarket, so we need to work quickly!"

"Joanie finished her gift a few days ago," explained Theresa. "With Grandmother's help, she was able to knit Mother a pretty red scarf. Now, she and Annie are putting their efforts into a birthday card. Annie hopes it will be the nicest birthday card Mother has ever seen."

J.M.J.

Theresa left Dad and went to the kitchen. "I'll help you, Tommy, to wrap your present!"

"Hi, Theresa, I picked some flowers for Tommy to give Mom for her birthday!" declared Annie.

"That was really generous of you, Annie, to help Tommy give a gift," declared Theresa. "Mom will be really pleased to have a gift from Tommy!"

"Are you going to make a cake, Theresa?" asked Annie.

"Yes, Annie, but I want you and Joanie to help me. We will let Johnny and Tommy help decorate it!"

"This is going to be a wonderful birthday for Mom," declared Annie with a loud happy shout.

Later that evening, after the family had a wonderful birthday party for Mom, Dad spoke to the children.

Health 3 for Young Catholics

57

"All you children have made your mom and me happy because you have given of yourselves to make this a happy day for both of us. You have given of your own time and effort. You have showed tremendous love and respect for us both.

"Jesus is happy tonight, Children, because of the respect and love you have shown for your parents. That is what makes God very happy. Just like your mom and I respect our parents, your grandparents, you have pleased Jesus through your respect for us.

"The Fourth Commandment tells us to respect and obey our parents. Respect for parents means more than obeying when you are asked," explained Father. "Respect means that when you have a choice to do something extra, you treat your parents very well. It mean not only being polite and not talking back; it also means being obedient the first time you are asked. It means doing nice extra things without being asked, like keeping your room clean or doing the dishes before you are asked. The other day, Johnny helped me take off my jacket when I hurt my arm, and Tommy carried my extra jacket to help! That was very thoughtful and respectful!"

"Respect for parents means that when you would like to go skating, and you see Mother working in the garden, you decide to stay home and help her. Respect for parents means doing things with cheerfulness and not with a moping face. Respect for parents means helping to teach a younger brother or sister, often by good example, or by showing kindness and even helping them with their studies.

"Respect for parents is a special gift, a gift of a lifetime, a gift that will be greatly rewarded in ways you can never imagine now. For now, just know that your respect is a huge gift, not only for your mom and dad, but also for Jesus, Who loves you very much for your gift of respect for the two people He has given you as parents. Children, your parents love you more than anyone in the world ever will or ever can.

"Now come here, all of you, so that Mom and I can both give you lots of hugs and kisses!"

## Lesson Review

1. Why is it good to exercise?

   _____

   _____

2. Why should you drink water after exercising?

   _____

   _____

3. Is it important to warm up before exercising?

   _____

4. What is good sportsmanship?

_____

_____

_____

5. What exercises do you do?

_____

_____

6. Do you exercise every day?

_____

7. What does respect mean?

_____

_____

8. Which Commandment tells us to respect and obey our parents?

_____

9. Why should I respect my parents?

_____

_____

## Activities

Check your heart rate! Here's what you will need:

- the cardboard tube from a paper towel roll, and
- a watch or clock with a second hand.

You can check your heart rate by using an empty paper towel roll the same way as a doctor uses a stethoscope. Go to a quiet area. Be sure you are calm and haven't been moving about too much. Ask Mom or Dad to put the paper towel roll next to your heart. Your parent will then listen to your heart, counting how many heart beats they hear in 30 seconds.

Double that number. Now you know how many times your heart beats each minute! This is your "resting" heart rate.

Next, do ten jumping jacks. Then ask your Mom or Dad to check your heart rate again. This is your "active" heart rate.

How are the numbers different?

# Chapter 7. Safety in the Home

Mrs. Martin was holding an ice pack to Johnny's head. Joanie was hurrying to the freezer to get more ice. As she put the ice in a bag, Joanie was fighting back the tears. It was awful to see her brother hurt, and she hoped he wouldn't need to go to the hospital.

"Please, dear Jesus, let Johnny be okay," she prayed.

Meanwhile, Theresa was cleaning up a few drops of her brother's blood off the kitchen floor.

It was five o'clock, and Father was just getting home from work. As he entered upon the kitchen scene, Father stopped and quickly examined Johnny's head. "It looks like the bleeding is going to stop soon. I think he'll be okay." Then he asked, "What happened here?"

Everyone was silent at first, then Mother spoke: "Johnny, would you like to tell Father what you did?"

The young boy hung his head. It was a few moments before he could bring himself to speak, "I hit my head on the kitchen counter."

Mr. Martin, seeing the blood on the counter said, "Yes, so it seems, but how did you do that?"

Johnny paused once more. His voice was now

barely a whisper, "I climbed up on the counter to reach the cookie jar. Then I slipped and fell." Johnny tried not to cry, but his head ached, and he was ashamed of what he had done.

"I'm sorry, Dad. I'm sorry, Mother." Johnny knew he was hurt because he had disobeyed his parents. "Please forgive me."

"Johnny, yes, of course, we forgive you. But you know we have rules about what you and the other children are allowed to do! The rules are to keep you safe. The rules are about what you and your brothers and sisters are allowed to do inside the house. The rules are to keep everyone safe and to prevent accidents. If someone disobeys one of the rules, that person and others may get hurt."

There was a moment of silence.

"After dinner, Mother, let's have a meeting and go over the rules for safety in the house," said Father.

Health 3 for Young Catholics

J.M.J.

Later, after the family finished dinner, Father asked that everyone come to a meeting in the family room. Everyone quietly walked to the family room and sat down.

"After Johnny's accident today," Father began, "I think we should review our house safety rules. Don't you agree, Mother?"

"Very definitely, Father!"

"Well, Theresa, since you are the oldest, would you like to start by mentioning one of our house safety rules?" asked Father.

"Okay, Dad. An important house safety rule is 'Do not run in the house!' And you have said we should not run in stores or in church either."

"That's right, Theresa!" responded Father, "Besides increasing the risk that you or others will get hurt, running at church or in stores also shows a lack of courtesy."

"Joanie, do you remember another house safety rule?" asked Father.

"Yes, Dad, and this is one I won't forget: Do not stand on furniture or kitchen counters. If we need to reach something, we should ask you or Mom to get it for us!"

"Very good, Joanie! Now, Johnny, would you like to think about another house rule we should follow?" asked Father.

64    Health 3 for Young Catholics

"Yes, Dad. We should be careful holding knives and scissors. We should carry scissors closed with the sharp point down. We should not carry a knife unless absolutely necessary. But if we do need to carry a knife, like when we are helping Mom set the table, we should keep the sharp point down."

"Very good, Johnny. I hope you will follow all these rules in the future! Now Annie, it is your turn. I know you are only five, but can you remember one of our house rules?" asked Father.

"Yes, Dad, the rule I remember is one that Mom often reminds me about: Never walk or run with a lollipop, food, or anything else in my mouth!"

"Very good, Annie! Okay, Tommy, you are only three, but do you remember a house rule?"

"I remember a rule: Keep little things away from Baby Rosie, because she might put them in her mouth and choke on them!" said Tommy.

"Very good, Tommy! Theresa, do you want to think of another house rule?" asked Father.

"Sure, Dad. I remember this one, because I help Mom in the kitchen:

Keep away from the stove until you are older! When I am helping Mom with the cooking, sometimes the little ones forget this rule!"

"Thank you Theresa, for helping your mother in the kitchen. You younger ones can help by staying away from the stove! It just might be hot. And it is important not to touch any of the dials on the stove," declared Father.

"Do you remember another rule, Joanie?" asked Father.

"Yes, Dad. This morning, I stepped on a plastic piece from a game, so I remember this rule: Do not leave toys, shoes, or small game pieces on the floor, where someone can step on them or stumble over them."

"I'm sorry, Joanie!" Annie said suddenly.

"Johnny, do you remember another house rule?" asked Father.

"Yes, Dad. We must not try to use machines in the kitchen, like the mixer, or machines in your workshop, like the drill, without having you or Mom help us," added Johnny.

"Very good, Johnny! Another house rule," began Dad, "is about something that is not a machine, but a ladder. Don't use a ladder until your Mom or I am around. Ladders can be dangerous; if you fall off, you could be seriously hurt! About a month ago, a teenage girl had to go to the hospital when she fell off a ladder as she was tacking up pictures on her bedroom wall!"

"Father," began Mother, " I think I should remind everyone about another house rule, about the medicine cabinet in the bathrooms."

"Yes, Mother, please go ahead and tell the children that rule," said Father.

"Children, never help yourselves to anything from the medicine cabinet, either for yourself or for another child. That is a job for your parents. If you were to swallow some medicine that is not for you, you could become very sick and might need to go to the hospital. Never, never, never take anyone else's medicine. If you need medicine, make sure you come and ask your Father or me to get it for you."

"I think I should also mention a few house rules that are really yard rules, for outside the house!" said Father.

"Stay away from all power tools," declared Father. "Lawnmowers and all other power tools run by gasoline or electricity. They are very dangerous tools and are made to be used only by adults. Stay away from gas cans. Also, do not go near an adult who is using a power tool, because he might not hear or see you, and you could get seriously hurt.

"And when you are climbing a tree or playing on something that you are climbing, make sure somebody can see you. That way, if you fall or get hurt, they can get help for you. Last week, you remember the boy who went in the woods by himself, and was swinging across the ravine, and fell and broke his leg? It took him a long time to get himself out of the woods before he could get help," explained Father.

"That reminds me," said Mother, "about an accident that happened last summer when school was out, but the neighborhood children were using the playground equipment. They were playing on the jungle gym and doing tricks they should not have been doing. A good rule, Children, is to use playground equipment the way it supposed to be used!"

Health 3 for Young Catholics

"Mother," said Father, "Another outside-the-house rule is this: Put away toys and bicycles after you finish with them. Do the same with rakes, shovels, and other tools. Someone could easily get hurt by the toys or tools that are hidden by the grass and cannot be seen when it starts to get dark! And never leave a bicycle or any toys behind a car, which might not be seen by the driver."

"One other thing, Children," said Father. "No one is to use the computer without permission. Also, the computer must remain here in the family room, where people are constantly going in and out. No one may remain alone in a room with the computer on, except for Mom or Dad."

"Well, I am sure now," said Mother quietly, "that everyone will remember these rules. But I think that tomorrow the children and I will write up a list. We can write them in colored pens and pencils, and put them on our corkboard in the kitchen so that we can be reminded of them every day. After today's accident, we don't want anyone else to get hurt!"

"Let's say a Hail Mary to thank Jesus and the Blessed Mother for protecting Johnny from being hurt more seriously. And let's pray to all the saints, especially each of our patron saints, and our guardian angels to protect all of us, and to help us remember to follow the safety rules."

## Lesson Review

1. What might happen if a child does not follow safety rules?

   _____

2. Where should you not run?

   _____

J.M.J.

3. Why should you keep small items away from babies?

_____

4. Why should you put away toys when you are finished playing with them?

_____

5. Why should you not get anything out of the medicine cabinet?

_____

_____

## Activities

*Emergency Phone List*

Does your family have a list of emergency numbers posted near the phone or on a cell phone? Some numbers that should be on your list are 911 (for all emergencies) and Poison Control (1-800-222-1222).

You can add the local police department, and important family or friends whom you might need to call for extra help if there is an emergency.

Consider making a list of household rules for your house. Use colored pens or pencils, and even add pictures if you wish.

## Did You Know?

About half of the children who go to the emergency room need to go because of some kind of fall, usually at home. Free home safety rules are available on the Internet. Free first-aid courses are available for parents and children at most fire stations or local hospitals.

Health 3 for Young Catholics

# Chapter 8. Fire Safety

"Oh, that's terrible!" said Mother, who was talking on the phone. "Thank goodness everyone is okay. How scary for them, though! Please tell them we are praying for them. Thank you. Good-bye."

"Who was it, Mother?" asked Theresa when her mother had hung up the phone.

"It was Mrs. Allen. She told me that her neighbor had a house fire last night. It is a family that goes to our church, the Murphy family. Everyone was able to get out in time, but their father breathed in a little too much smoke. He is in the hospital recovering. He will be fine. They won't be able to live in their house anymore, though. We must think of a way we can help them."

"How sad," said Theresa. "Do you know how it happened?"

"They think it had something to do with the fireplace. Fortunately, the smoke detectors went off and let them know they needed to get out quickly," said Mother.

"Mother, they must have lost a lot of things in the fire. Can we help by collecting clothes for them?" asked Joanie.

"That's a wonderful idea! I was hoping we could help. That is the perfect answer!" exclaimed Mother.

Mother started making phone calls, organizing a collection of clothes. The children scattered around the house, looking for toys and clothes that they could give to the Murphy family.

At dinner that evening, Father spoke about fire.

"Fire is one of God's gifts to us, but it needs great care. Fires help us to keep warm and to cook. However, fire can become very dangerous if it is not used in the right way."

"Dad," said Theresa, "maybe we should have a family meeting about preventing fires in the house!"

"Theresa, that is a very good idea! After dinner, let's meet in the family room and have a discussion about preventing fires," declared Father.

After everyone finished dinner and cleaned up in the kitchen, the whole family went to the family room.

"Okay, Children, let's think of some important rules for fire safety," encouraged Father. "Theresa, what do you think is the most important rule we should talk about with regard to preventing a fire in our home?"

"I think the most important rule is never to play with matches, lighters, or lit candles," declared Theresa. "I remember hearing about an eight-year-old boy from our church who played with matches while hiding in the bathroom. He set the curtains on fire. His mother smelled smoke and was able to put out the fire. They were fortunate that the whole house didn't burn down!"

"That is a basic rule, Theresa," said Father. "Even when we lose electricity, we are very careful to use flashlights or battery-powered lanterns, nothing with fire or matches, and certainly not candles. Last year, I purchased several solar rechargeable LED night-light lanterns. We now have them throughout the house. They are easy to use for everyone. Just in case, however, I have one here in the bookcase. Let's take turns with everyone learning how to turn it on."

Dad gave everyone an opportunity to turn on the lantern. It seemed a little tricky for Tommy, but he learned how to do it.

"Okay, Joanie, what rule do you suggest for preventing a fire?"

"Well, we have a smoke detector right on the wall in here!" declared Joanie. "And there is another one in the kitchen, and one at the top of the stairs!"

"Yes, Joanie, and I put another one in the garage. I purchased them two years ago. They are battery operated, so I should check all the batteries again to make sure they will work. The batteries should be checked twice a year. It is important to have them on the wall," stated Father, "because we want them to detect smoke before it reaches the ceiling. The firemen say they should be placed between 4 inches and 12 inches below the ceiling."

"Dad, could I look a little closer at the smoke detector?" asked Johnny. I want to see if I can find out how it works!"

"Okay, Johnny, go look at it. Then come back and take your turn. Can you think of any other rules for fire prevention or safety?" asked Father.

"Well, we have a fire extinguisher in the kitchen!" remembered Johnny. "It is sitting on the wall near the stove!"

"Very good, Johnny! You are pretty familiar with the kitchen, I see!" responded Father. "Yes, fire extinguishers are important. They are for putting out a fire, of course, rather than preventing a fire. But they do prevent a fire from spreading!"

"Father, should you tell the children how to use a fire extinguisher?" asked Mother.

"Good point, Mother! Let me bring it in and we can talk about it." Father left to get the fire extinguisher from the kitchen. He returned a moment later.

"All right, Children!" said Father. "Notice the instructions are on the side. As you can see, we need to pull this ring, and then stand back from the fire. You should stand back from the fire about seven feet, which means about a foot more than how tall I am!"

"Let's measure that, Father!" exclaimed mother. "Let me walk seven feet so that the younger children can see the distance," explained Mother. "I will take seven foot-long steps!"

"Okay, Mother! We can even go into the kitchen and stand back seven feet from the stove, which would be the most likely place for a fire in the kitchen. Let's go!"

The family followed Father into the kitchen. "Okay, Children! Once you are back seven feet, you squeeze the lever and use the hose, spraying the fire from side to side, like this, as I show you."

"Father, let's go outside so that you can show the children exactly how it works!" proclaimed Mother.

"Okay, let's go outside the house, and I will show you how it works!"

Father walked out the kitchen door, followed by Mother and the children. Father read the directions on the fire extinguisher.

"Okay, now I am going to demonstrate how to use the fire extinguisher. Step back!"

Father pulled the lever, and the spray came out, and Father moved it side to side, seven feet back from the bushes.

"It is very easy to use! Here, Teresa, come and use it. Each one of you older children can practice using it. I can buy another one to replace this one."

After each took a turn, Father asked the children to come back to the family room.

"One thing we can do is look online," Father continued, "and I will find a video that explains how to use a fire extinguisher. That will help us to remember. Also, our fire department has days when they offer training for people, including children, about how to use a fire extinguisher. So, Mother, we need to call the fire department and find out when the next one is scheduled for children."

"One other thing, Children," Father continued. "We don't need to go over the rules now for putting out a campfire, but the next time we go camping, we need to have a practice. You remember last summer when we used both water and dirt to make sure our campfire was completely out. That is very important! Forest fires can cause terrible destruction, not only for the forest, but also for many homes and families. Sometimes, of course, forest fires are started by lightning. We need to remember in our prayers those families whose homes are in danger from forest fires," explained Father.

"Father, I think we should talk about what to do in case one of the children gets caught in a fire while in the house," suggested Mother.

"Yes, we do need to talk about what you children need to do so that you can get out of a fire safely!" stated Father.

"We should pray that we never have a fire in our house!" shouted Tommy.

"Yes, Tommy, you are right! The very best thing to do is to never have a fire, and praying for that is very important. Tommy, please do keep that in your nightly prayers!"

"Okay, Dad!"

"Well," continued Father, "just in case you ever are in any location where there is a fire, the most important thing to remember is to get

Health 3 for Young Catholics

down on your knees or even on your stomach, and crawl along on the floor as low as possible. Since smoke rises in the air, the least amount of smoke is next to the floor."

"Well, Dad, I can crawl and slide on the floor like a snake," declared Tommy.

"That is exactly what you need to do, Tommy: crawl or slide on your tummy on the floor like a snake!"

"What people don't realize," Mother added, "is that most people don't die from the fire; they die from breathing the smoke! That is what Mr. Turner, the fireman, said."

"And while you are sliding along the floor, feel for the exit door. If the door is hot, or the handle of the door is hot, don't go through the door. Do not open the door, I repeat," said Dad firmly, "because if you open the door, the air in your room will give the fire more strength. You need to consider another exit, or get to a window and scream out the window for help!"

"Another thing to remember," said Mother, "is do not hide. If a fireman is looking for you, he might not be able to find you if you are hiding under a bed. The smoke and fire might find you, but the fireman might not be able to find you!"

"That's a good point, Mother!" emphasized Father. "Get out as quickly as you can, but do not put yourself in a worse situation. We can draw maps showing two ways to get out of each room. These are called Emergency Fire Exit Maps, and they are required at places where people work."

"Can I help draw one for my bedroom?" asked Johnny.

"Yes, Johnny, that is a great idea. You will remember it better if you help draw it. We will try to find two different ways to get out of your bedroom in case of a fire."

"Well," said Mother, "one important way to escape from an upstairs fire is by using a long heavy rope."

"A rope is good, but now," Dad explained, "because so many people die in fires on the second floor of their homes, we can buy Fire Escape Ladders for children!"

"Wow! Dad," exclaimed Johnny, "let's go buy some of those tomorrow! I want to practice with one of those!"

"Actually, Johnny, that is a great idea!" admitted Father. "The statistics are that more people die on second and third floors of a building because they cannot escape. It is estimated that 80 percent of the people who die in a house fire die because they cannot escape from an upper floor!"

"When I was at the fire station a year ago learning about the fire trucks," explained Teresa, "I remember the fireman talking about a strong fabric rope with a hook at the top to fit over the window sill. They have light fire escape ropes, especially for children."

"Father," started Mother, "I think we should get one of those fire escape ladders for each room upstairs. And we need the children to practice using them!"

Health 3 for Young Catholics

J.M.J.

"I will purchase enough fire escape ladders for each room upstairs, Mother!"

"Dad," Joanie began, "what should we do if our clothes catch on fire?"

"Okay, Joanie, that is an important question! What do we do if our clothes catch on fire? Here is the answer. This is what the fire fighters say to do: stop, drop, and roll!"

"If you or your clothing catches on fire," continued Dad, "the best thing to do is to stop, drop to the ground or floor, cover your face, and roll. Fire needs air to breathe. If you run around, it will give the fire more air, and the fire will get larger! If you roll on the ground, the ground will smother the fire, and it will go out. You should cover your face when you roll to protect your face from the fire. Practice this: stop, drop, and roll."

"Can we practice now, Dad?" asked Tommy.

"Okay, Tommy, that is a good idea! Let's get on the floor, kids, and I will watch you. Remember, stop, drop, and roll!"

Everyone got down on the floor, and Dad watched as each child covered his or her face, and rolled to put out the imaginary fire.

J.M.J.

"Okay, kids, let's review the rules again: If your clothes are on fire, do not run and do not try to pat out the flames. Drop down, lying on your stomach. Close your eyes and cover your face and mouth with your hands to protect yourself from the fire and smoke. Roll onto your back and onto your front, back and forth until the flames are put out.

"Remember, fire needs air, and you are trying to smother the flames. As quickly as possible, remove the burned clothes; they could start burning again. Put cool water on any burns you may have."

"Well, we definitely need to practice all these things, Father," declared Mother. "There is one other thing we need to remember and practice: the exact location where we need to meet outside the house when each person gets out. Sometimes parents worry about a missing child, and the child is out of the house in the backyard, while mom and dad are in the front yard!"

"That is a good point, Mother," declared Father. "When we have our practices for the fire drills, we need to remember to gather together outside on the front sidewalk! We cannot endanger the life of a fireman looking for a child who is already out of the house!"

"Okay, Children, it's bedtime! Let's head upstairs and get a good night's sleep, and we will have a fire practice this weekend with a good fire ladder."

Health 3 for Young Catholics

## Lesson Review

1. Name three things that every home should have for fire safety?

   _____

   _____

2. What should you do if you are in a smoky room?

   _____

   _____

3. What should you do if you or your clothes catch on fire?

   _____

   _____

4. Do you have a rope ladder in each room upstairs?

   _____

## Activities

*Escape Route*

Mom and Dad will show you a plan in case of a fire in your home. Knowing how to escape from a fire in your home is very important. Have you ever seen maps in public buildings showing the best way out? Make something similar to this for your home. Draw a map of your home. Include all levels and all rooms. If possible, visit each room of your home. Draw all windows and doors. On your map, label where each smoke detector is located. If you have fire extinguishers, include them in your drawing as well. You may use symbols for these items if you wish. Decide with your family where your outside meeting place will be. Include this as well. Everyone in the family should be aware of the rules and the escape routes, and the place to meet outside the house. The entire family can discuss the best ways out of the house. Post your map somewhere in your home where you can review it often.

## Did You Know?

There is a special novena to St. Joseph to protect us from many things, including being burned in a fire. This is a very old novena that was found only 50 years after the birth of Christ. It is said that whoever reads it or carries it shall never die a sudden death or be burned in any fire.

## Novena to St. Joseph

O Saint Joseph, whose protection is so great, so strong, so prompt before the Throne of God, I place in you all my interests and desires.

O Saint Joseph, assist me by your powerful intercession and obtain for me from your Divine Son all spiritual blessings through Jesus Christ, Our Lord; so that, having engaged here below your heavenly power, I may offer my thanksgiving and homage to the most loving of Fathers.

O Saint Joseph, I never weary contemplating you and Jesus asleep in your arms; I dare not approach while He reposes near your heart. Press Him in my name and kiss His fine head for me, and ask Him to return the Kiss when I draw my dying breath. Amen.

O Saint Joseph, hear my prayers and obtain my petitions. O Saint Joseph, pray for me. (Mention your special intention.)

# Chapter 9. Strangers and a Word of Caution

"Okay, Children, would you like to talk about our vacation?"

Father had asked Mother and the children to gather on Sunday afternoon in the family room. Once they were seated, Dad asked the question.

Tommy instantly asked, "Daddy, when are we going to leave for our vacation?"

"I need a drink of water first, Daddy," declared Annie.

"Okay, everybody, get a drink and a cookie and come back here," said Father, "and then we can settle down so that we can all talk about our vacation plans!"

Everyone scurried back to the kitchen for a drink and a homemade chocolate-chip cookie!

"Where are we going, Dad?" asked Theresa when she returned.

"We are going to our nation's capital, Washington, D.C.," answered Father. "And, to answer Annie, we will leave the third week of June, after you all have finished your homeschooling assignments!"

"Wow!" exclaimed Johnny as he sat down. "I want to visit Mount Vernon, George Washington's home. Mother told us about his home. He was our first president! And I want to visit the Washington Monument!"

"Father," Theresa said, "We must visit the Jefferson Memorial and the Lincoln Memorial, and of course, the White House."

"Okay, okay. We'll include all those on our trip."

J.M.J.

"Do they have a zoo in Washington, Dad?" asked little Annie.

"I think they do, Annie. We will be sure to visit the zoo while we are there."

Mother became thoughtful, and then she spoke.

"This is going to take a lot of planning to visit all the places we want to see in Washington, our nation's capital city. And we will be doing a lot of walking around."

"That's okay, Mom! I will help take care of the children!" announced Theresa.

"I know you will, Theresa," admitted Mom, "but we definitely need to talk about certain rules while we are visiting all these places."

"Your mother is right, Children. Washington is a large and busy city, with hundreds, maybe even thousands, of visitors there. We will be

Health 3 for Young Catholics

traveling to a place that none of you has ever visited before. You could easily get lost in a crowd just by walking down the street during the busy time of the day. Now is a good time to remind you about how you are to behave while on vacation."

"We'll be good, Mom," declared Joanie.

"I know you all will be good, but I am concerned that we all stay together," Mom declared, "and that no one gets lost!"

"Well, Mother, you should tell the children the rules to follow so that they don't get lost!" declared Father. "Or, perhaps I should say, so that we don't lose anyone!"

"When we are out sightseeing," began Mother, "you must stay close to your father and me. All of you must be holding someone's hand at all times. I want each of you to keep an eye on your brothers and sisters. Always be sure everyone is together. Of course, Dad and I will be carrying Rosie, or pushing her in the stroller. One of us will be holding Tommy's hand. Theresa, you can walk with Johnny. Joanie, you can walk with Annie. We all need to be looking out for one another. I want everyone to be in sight at all times. I don't want anyone missing at any time."

"You are right, Mother," Father agreed. "No one should wander off by himself. You could easily get lost in the crowd. However, if that does happen, remember this rule: Look for someone who can help you find us."

"Let me repeat what I just said, Children," repeated Dad. "If you get lost, look for someone to help you find us. If it happens in a store or a museum, go to someone close by who works there. Look for a name tag, so that you are sure the person works there. In a museum, you can go to someone who is working at one of the information counters or look for a guard. If for some reason, you can't find any of these people, or if we are outdoors, look for a mother who is with her children. If you see a police officer, of course, tell him you are lost."

"Look for a mother who is with her children!" Mother said.

After a few seconds of quiet thinking, Mother continued. "Father," she said, "I think we should have each child, one by one, explain what he or she would do if lost."

"That is a good idea, Mother! In fact, we can drill all these rules in the car, several times, before we get there!"

"Well," said Theresa, "all of us should know your cell phone numbers. Maybe you could write them down for the younger children, Mom."

"That is a good idea, Theresa. Sometimes in the excitement, it is hard to remember phone numbers. So we can write the phone numbers on a card, and our address also. You children should keep this information in your pockets."

J.M.J.

"I don't like to say this," Dad began, "but all children need to be careful when they are traveling or when they are in a location where they don't know people. There are some people who offer candy, money, or games to children. The person might ask you to help him or her with something. But if a stranger starts to talk to you and you are by yourself, do not answer that person. Run away and return to Mom's or Dad's side."

"These are very important rules, Children," Father said, "and they must be obeyed for your own safety."

"Listen to your Father, Children!" Mother said.

"Children," Father continued. "We have been talking about safety rules while we are on vacation. They are good rules. However, we must practice safety rules at home too."

"Yes, Father is right about that," declared Mother. "At home, make certain you know the person at the door before you open it. If you don't know who it is, have either Mother or Father answer the door. If neither of us is at home, and Theresa does not know who it is, do not open the door, and the person will go away. Remember, no matter what they say, do not open the door," Mother warned.

"We should practice safety rules with the telephone, too," reminded Father. "Do not give out information to the caller, such as whether Mother or Father is not home. It is best not to talk to strangers on the phone. If the phone rings, let Mom or Dad answer it. If we are not available, then do not answer the phone at all; the caller can leave a message on our voice mail. Besides, Mom and I both have cell phones, so it really isn't necessary to answer the house phone anyway."

"And I am sure you children all know the emergency phone number," reminded Mother, "It's 911! Do not hesitate to call that number if you are in trouble and need help from the police."

"It was on the news last week, Mother," said Theresa, "that there was a little four-year-boy who took the cell phone and hid in a closet when a stranger walked in his house. He called 911 while he was hiding in the closet!"

"He was pretty smart!" declared Johnny loudly.

"Listen to Mother," continued Father. "She loves you children and knows what is best for you. There are other important safety rules in our home. Do not turn on the television or play a video game without our permission. Never go on the Internet without permission either. Sometimes bad people can try to trick you when you are using the Internet. If we know what you are doing, we can protect you from these people," Father explained.

"Sometimes," Johnny said, "a friend asks me to go to his house, but I am not sure whether I should go."

"You are right about that, Johnny," said Dad. "Never enter any home without our permission. If we do not know the parents in that house, or if the parents are not home, we will not give our permission. And I am sure you all know this rule: Never, never accept a car ride from a stranger, and never get close to a stranger's car."

"Remember, Children, no one loves you more than your mother and your father," Mother declared. "Never keep secrets from your parents. We want to keep you safe from harm. If you keep secrets from us, we will not be able to help you if you are in danger."

"We have talked a lot about a number of safety rules," Father said. "Remember that your guardian angels are always with you, and that your patron saints are also looking out for you. Of course, Jesus, Mary, and Joseph are looking out for you as well. So, whenever you think you might be in danger, or when you need special help or protection, say a prayer and ask for help and protection. Your guardian angels are always by your side. They want you to call upon them when you are in need or in possible

Health 3 for Young Catholics

J.M.J.

danger. They love you because Jesus sent them to take care of you. Always ask your angels to help you."

"Let's say the Guardian Angel prayer, Children," suggested Mother, "just to remind ourselves that when we are on vacation, we will need our guardian angels to protect us, more than when we are at home! Let's say it together!"

"Angel of God, my guardian dear, to whom God's love commits me here. Ever this day, be at my side, to light and guard, to rule and guide. Amen."

## Lesson Review

1. Why should you stay close to your parents when you are out?

2. To whom should you go if you are lost?

3. If a stranger talks to you when you are not close to a parent, what should you do?

4. Should you ever go close to a stranger's car?

5. What are some things in your home that you should not use without asking your parents' permission first?

6. Recite the Guardian Angel prayer and print it here.

_____

_____

## Activities

*Know Your Phone Number and Address*

Do you know your parents' phone numbers? Do you know your address? If not, take some time now to memorize them. Repeat them every day to be sure you do not forget them. However, sometimes when you are frightened, you might forget your phone number and address. Have them written down on an index card, and keep this index card in your pocket.

*Safety-Rules Drawing*

Read the safety rules in this chapter again. Draw a picture showing at least one of the rules. If you want to do more pictures, fold the paper in half. Fold it in half again. Open the paper. You should now have four sections on your paper. Choose four rules to illustrate. Draw one in each section of your paper. This will help you to remember the rules.

## Did You Know?

9-1-1 is the emergency number for the United States and Canada. Other countries, however, have different emergency numbers. Many countries in Europe, like Italy, Spain, and France, use 1-1-2 as their emergency number. If you're in England, you would dial 9-9-9. If you live in Australia, you would dial 0-0-0; in New Zealand, you would dial 1-1-1. In Mexico, it is 0-6-6. So, if you are ever traveling to a different country, be sure to find out what that country's emergency number is before you visit there!

# Chapter 10. Health and Table Manners

"Children, dinner will be ready in 15 minutes!"

Joanie and Johnny were in the backyard playing with the volleyball when they heard their mom call.

They quickly answered, "Yes, Mom. We're going to get ready right now."

"Come on, Johnny. Let's hurry."

They ran inside and upstairs to the bathroom.

"You wash up first, Johnny. I'll get a clean blouse."

Johnny washed his hands and face. Then he noticed that his shirt was covered with dirt from the volleyball, so he changed into a clean one.

As Johnny was going downstairs, he heard his mother's voice giving the same directions she gives to everyone before dinner every night: "Please be sure you wash your hands before putting anything on the table."

"I know, Mom. My hands need to be clean, and I must handle the silverware by the handles, not by the part that we put in our mouths. I'll put out the knives, forks, and spoons, and I will put them on the clean paper napkins that Annie put on the table, and not on the tablecloth," Joanie said.

"Thank you, Joanie," said Mom from the kitchen.

J.M.J.

"I washed my hands, and I will put the dishes and glasses on the table," Theresa said. "I will pour the milk, and the water for Dad."

"I washed my hands, Mom!" declared Johnny. "So I will put on the potatoes and corn."

"Great, Johnny!" declared Mom.

"Hi, everyone!" announced Dad, as he walked into the dining room. "How's dinner coming along."

"We're doing fine, Father," said Mother, "but would you please get Rosie from the family room, and put her in her high chair?"

"Sure, I'll do that!" declared Father.

"And when you return, would you please put the meat on the table? I am making the gravy."

Health 3 for Young Catholics

Finally, the table was set. The meal was ready quickly because everyone had pitched in to help. All the children sat down at the table. Father waited until Mother sat down at the table.

"Everyone seated?" Father asked. "Fine, let's say grace. Johnny, do you want to lead us tonight?"

"Sure, Dad! In the name of the Father, and of the Son, and of the Holy Spirit. Bless us, O Lord, and these Thy gifts, which we are about to receive from Thy bounty, through Christ Our Lord. Amen."

After the food was passed around, and everyone started eating, Dad said, "Children, I was thinking about Saint Dominic Savio when we were saying grace. Once, when Saint Dominic Savio was a little boy, a friend of his father came for dinner. The man began eating without first saying grace. Little Dominic made the suggestion that they say grace first. Dominic knew that everyone needs to show gratitude to God for the food He so lovingly provides. Whether we are at home or eating at a restaurant, we always should say grace before meals."

J.M.J.

"One time, I was at Susie's house for lunch," said Joanie, "and they did not say grace at all. I just said it quietly to myself."

"That is best, Joanie," declared Father, "because as a guest, you don't want anyone to feel uncomfortable. But sometime you might invite her here for lunch, and she can see that we say grace."

"Tommy, please chew with your mouth closed," Mother reminded. "Food must be chewed slowly and carefully before swallowing. For good health, you don't want your stomach to struggle to digest your food. You might get a stomach ache."

"Annie," said Father. "I see you are struggling with your knife. We cut food by first holding the fork in the left hand. We place our forefinger along the back of the fork. The knife is held in a similar way in our right hand. The food is pierced by the fork to keep it from moving. The knife in our right hand cuts the pieces."

Mrs. Martin then asked, "Tommy, did you forget what to do with your napkin?"

"Oops," said Tommy. Tommy unfolded the napkin and placed it on his lap as Mother had taught him.

Annie suddenly jumped up from the table.

"Annie," Father said, "Don't you remember our rule about getting up from the table when we are eating?"

"I remember," said Johnny. "If we ever want to leave the table, we must first ask to be excused."

"May I please be excused to wash my hands?" Annie asked? "I spilled gravy on them."

Health 3 for Young Catholics

93

"You have permission, Annie," Father said. "It is important for good health, Children, to keep your hands clean and not to eat with your fingers, at any time, if at all possible. If you are going to a picnic or a similar outside event, carry some hand sanitizer wipes in your pocket."

"I see that you children are eating all the food on your plate," Father noted. "That is really great! God does not want us to waste any food which He has kindly provided for us. We have talked in the past about how we must not complain if we do not like the taste of the food. That would be very unkind to your mother, who has spent so much time to prepare and cook it."

Mother continued, "It is good to remember that there are many people throughout the world who do not have enough to eat. There are many children who go to bed hungry every night. We should be grateful that we have enough food to eat, even if it is not our favorite. And it is wrong to waste food."

"There is another rule we should remember," declared Father. "We must wait to swallow our food before speaking. It is not polite, and it does not look nice at all, to speak with food in your mouth!"

"Father, maybe this is a good time to go over some of the other rules for eating a meal at the table," said Mother, "especially since we will be visiting our relatives in Ohio next month."

"Well, Children, let's go around the table, and each one of us can think of a rule for eating at the table," declared Father.

"Well," started Theresa, "We are not supposed to have our elbows on the table!"

"And," said Joanie, "we are not supposed to argue or shout at the table! And we are not to interrupt when someone else is speaking!" declared Joanie with a meaningful look at her brother Johnny.

"We should not wipe our mouth on our sleeves," squealed little Tommy. "I remember that one from last week when you told me!"

"Also," added Annie, "we are not allowed to play with our food on the plate! And I know who likes to do that with his peas!"

"I know another one, Dad," Tommy declared quickly. "We must ask politely for a second helping! Dad, may I please have some more mashed potatoes?"

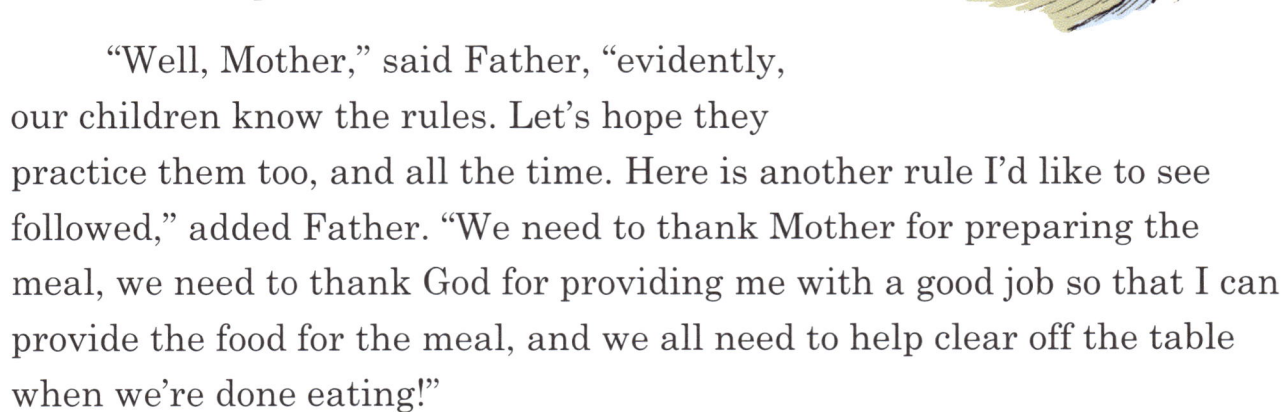

"Well, Mother," said Father, "evidently, our children know the rules. Let's hope they practice them too, and all the time. Here is another rule I'd like to see followed," added Father. "We need to thank Mother for preparing the meal, we need to thank God for providing me with a good job so that I can provide the food for the meal, and we all need to help clear off the table when we're done eating!"

"Thank you, Mother, for a delicious meal!" continued Father. "Let's bow our heads, Children. We give Thee thanks for our wonderful dinner, Almighty God," began Father, "Who lives and reigns forever. And may the souls of the faithful departed through the mercy of God, rest in peace. Amen."

"Whose turn is it to do the dishes?" asked Johnny. "I know it's not mine!"

## Lesson Review

1. What should we always do before beginning to eat?

_____

Health 3 for Young Catholics

J.M.J.

2. Where should your napkin be placed while you are eating?

   _____

3. What bothered Saint Dominic Savio when a guest came for dinner?

   _____

4. If you must leave the table, what should you first ask?

   _____

5. Why should you eat everything on your plate?

   _____

## Activities

*Set the Table*

There is a picture of a place setting in this chapter. It is a simple, everyday table setting. For fancier meals, more forks, spoons, or glasses might be needed. Practice setting a simple place at the table like the one in the picture. You could save this activity for dinner time to be an extra big help.

> "Therefore, whether you eat or drink, or whatsoever else you do, do all to the glory of God." (1 Corinthians 10:31)

## Did You Know?

Long ago, in fifteenth-century England, table manners were very different from today. Men wore their hats at the table so that their long hair would stay out of their food. Food was eaten with the fingers; there was no silverware, and there were no napkins! Long ago, people did not know about germs.

J.M.J.

# Chapter 11. Being Helpful and Being Thankful

Joanie and Johnny were up before sunrise. They were going fishing with Father and Uncle Mark.

"Be quiet, Children," whispered Father. "Let's tiptoe quietly out of the house so that we don't wake up anyone."

"This is going to be fun!" declared Joanie to Johnny.

"We need to get going, now, Mark, so that we can make the fishing boat on time," Father said.

Everyone climbed into the car. Uncle Mark sat in front with Dad. Dad started the engine, and he began driving down the road.

"Everything is so beautiful this early in the morning," Uncle Mark noted. "As the sun is coming up, it sheds a strange but beautiful yellow light on the green trees, the cows, horses, and even goats along the way."

They were on the road only about fifteen minutes when they saw a car parked on the side of the road. "Oh, dear!" Uncle Mark said, "Somebody is having trouble with his car."

"Yes. We need to stop and see if they are okay." Father slowed down the car and pulled up just ahead of the broken-down car on the side of the road.

"Mark, would you please get out and see if they need help?" asked Father.

"Sure!" Uncle Mark got out of the car and walked back to the parked car. He started talking with the driver.

"But, Dad," Johnny exclaimed, "we'll be late for the fishing boat. It will leave without us! Can't they wait for someone else to help them?"

J.M.J.

"Johnny, what if we were the ones stuck on the side of the road? Wouldn't you want someone to come and help us right away?" asked Father. "You two wait here in the car. They seem to be having a lot of conversation."

Father got out of the car. Joanie and Johnny waited in the car and watched as Father and Uncle Mark spoke to the two people. The woman was trying to get out of the car, but she was having a hard time. The young man reached into the back of the car and pulled out a pair of crutches. He handed them to the woman as he helped her get out. As the children watched, they saw that the woman had only one leg.

Then they saw Father and Uncle Mark lift the hood of the car. Smoke was pouring out. Father and Uncle Mark took out tools from the trunk of the car. They bent over the engine and started to work on it.

"What are they doing, I wonder?" said Joanie. "Do you think they will make the car work again?"

"I don't know! It seems awfully smoky to me! Maybe something is burning up!"

"I think maybe we are not going to be on time for the fishing boat! I think we might have to go fishing another time, Johnny," Joanie told her brother somewhat sadly.

"Yes, I guess we will wait and go fishing another time," Johnny agreed sadly.

About twenty minutes later, Dad and Uncle Mark got back in the car.

"Well, I'm sorry about that for you two," Father said. "We are too late to meet the fishing boat! But when someone is in trouble, we need to help, even when we have something important we want to do."

"Yes," explained Uncle Mark. "We should treat everyone in the same way that we would like to be treated. God made each of us different, but He loves us all equally the same. We must care about one another in the same way that God cares about us. When people are in trouble, we must help them if we want to be good Christians. After all, we are all His children!"

"Well, that is certainly true in our own family," admitted Johnny. "We are each different in some way. Some of us have blond hair, and some of us have brown hair."

"Although there are differences in the way we all look, we must remember that God made each and every one of us," explained Father. "All of us, no matter how different we appear, are children of our first parents, Adam and Eve. We are all members of the human family. We must follow Our Lord's command to "Love one another!""

"When we see a person who is in a wheelchair," Uncle Mark started to explain, "or when someone has a problem that keeps that person from being able to do things like us, we should go out of our way to be kind and helpful to that person. If you see someone with a problem or a handicap, say a little prayer for that person, who has daily struggles."

"Do you remember the story of Blessed Margaret of Castello?" questioned Dad. "She was blind, crippled, and even deformed when she was born. Yet, Margaret was a cheerful child. Despite all her problems,

J.M.J.

Margaret grew to be a very kind young woman. She did not focus on her own problems, but rather decided to help those who needed help—the poor and the sick. She forgave those who were unkind to her, and she prayed for them all. The Catholic Church is preparing to declare Blessed Margaret a saint in Heaven. Let us think of Blessed Margaret's kindness when we meet people who look different from us or who have problems."

"Sometimes," said Uncle Mark, "a playmate may be unkind, but we should not be unkind in return. We should remember the words of Jesus on the Cross: "Father, forgive them." We, too, must forgive if we want to be like Jesus. Good Catholic children try to see Jesus in the face of everyone they meet."

"Let's say a Rosary on our way back home and pray for that family we helped, and others on the road today who might need help!" Father said.

"I will start with the Act of Contrition!" declared Uncle Mark. Then, for the next fifteen minutes, they all said the Rosary.

When the children returned home, they told their mother what had happened.

"When we think about people who need our help," Mother reminded the children, "we can think about old Mrs. Simon down the street. I am so happy that you children go to visit her."

"She makes cookies for us, Mom!" Theresa reminded her. "And sometimes I help her knead the dough when she wants to bake bread!"

"Johnny and I sometimes help too!" said Joanie. "Johnny

helps pull out the weeds for Mrs. Simon, and I help rake the leaves. During the winter, we help shovel the snow from her sidewalk!"

"I am so glad you children realize the importance of caring for those who need help, especially older people!" explained Mrs. Martin, "I am glad you are willing to make the effort to help. I know that you took Annie to her house so that she could give her flowers last week. I also thank you, Theresa, for helping the younger children with their schoolwork and music lessons."

"And I congratulate Annie and Tommy, who pitch in and help when they can by picking up their toys and throwing away the trash," declared Father.

"And a special thank-you to Joanie for helping with Tommy and Rosie," said Mother.

"Even Tommy, though he is only three years old, does little chores around the house," said Father, "and he tries to be helpful. Helping one another at home and helping those outside our family are what Jesus expects us all to do. Jesus said, 'Love one another as I have loved you.' He also said, 'Love your neighbor as yourself!'"

"I remember last summer, Father," said Mother, "when you were mowing the lawn on a very hot day. Johnny took out a glass of water for you! Remember? And I remember the other children going out and moving the lawn furniture and toys out of the way to make your job easier, Father!"

Health 3 for Young Catholics

"Yes, I remember. Thanks again, Children! Our Lord wants us to help one another," Father explained. "Jesus said, 'For I was hungry and you gave Me food, I was thirsty and you gave Me drink, I was a stranger and you welcomed Me….'"

"When His disciples asked Him when they did all these things for Him, Jesus answered, 'Truly, I say to you, as you did it to one of the least of these My brethren, you did it to Me.' Our Lord is telling us that whatever good we do for someone, it will be as if we did it for Jesus. He created each one of us, and He wants us to help one another."

"Children, I'd like you to remember four important things about helping others," said Father.

"First, when you help others cheerfully, it makes you feel good inside. Knowing you are doing the right thing usually makes you feel this way. It is because you know you are making Jesus happy that you feel happier.

"Second, every person's job in our family is important. When you do your best to do your part, you help to make our home run smoothly and be a happy place.

"Third, when we help others, it makes us think less of ourselves. This helps us not to be selfish.

"Fourth, it is much easier to help someone if you think of the person as someone whom Jesus loves, just like He loves you. Whatever good you do to help others makes Jesus happy."

## Being Thankful

"When we can be helpful to others, we also realize that we must be thankful for all the gifts Jesus has given us and our family!" Dad proclaimed to the family one Sunday afternoon.

J.M.J.

"Here we are," Dad explained, "getting ready to go to St. John the Baptist Church's annual picnic at the lake. You will be having lots of fun. You will be playing volleyball and softball. Rowboats will be waiting to take you out on the lake. Hikers can explore the woods on the trails. You have packed lots of food and goodies! But have you thought about the many children in the world, and those even in our own city, who cannot ever go to a picnic or have lots of food and fun at a park?"

There was a moment of silence as the children thought about what Dad said. Then Mother spoke.

"God is so good to our family. Look at all He has given us. We must thank God every day for all the blessings we have!"

"Maybe we can list our blessings," suggested Dad, "before we leave for the picnic. Maybe we can thank God for everything He has done for us!"

"Well," said Theresa, "we can thank God for our good health, for our good weather, for our good home, for our friends, and for our house."

"We can thank God for our good food," said Johnny.

"We can thank God for Grandma and Grandpa," said Joanie.

Annie slowly started speaking. "Is it okay to thank God for ice cream and cake, and for our toys?"

"I thank God that I didn't need stitches when I banged my head," Johnny remembered.

104

Health 3 for Young Catholics

J.M.J.

"It is so important to be thankful for all we have, Children," reminded Father. "The best thing we have is our Catholic Faith. Being a member of the Catholic Church is another great gift for which to thank Jesus. We should take time each day to look at the world around us, and thank God for all that He lovingly provides for all of us."

"Before we leave," suggested Mother, "let's take the time to say a Rosary, not only to thank God for all our blessings, but also to pray that everyone will be safe at the picnic!"

"That is a good idea, Mother!" declared Father. "Let's all gather in the family room and say a Rosary! And let's remember Blessed Mother Teresa of Calcutta who dedicated her life to caring for poor children!"

## Lesson Review

1. How should we treat others?

   _____

2. Whom does God want us to love?

   _____

3. What did Blessed Margaret do instead of thinking of herself?

   _____

4. If someone is unkind to us, what should we do?

   _____

Health 3 for Young Catholics

J.M.J.

5. Name a way that you can be helpful at your home.

6. What does Our Lord want us to do?

7. Why do you feel happy when you do the right thing?

8. Name some things your parents have given you for which you are thankful.

9. Name something that God has given you for which you are thankful.

10. Should you always be looking for something else that you could have?

11. What can you do to show your parents that you are grateful to them?

## Activities

*"Truly, I say to you, as you did it to one of the least of these My brethren, you did it to Me." (Matthew 25:40)*

Talk with your mother or father about someone who is in need in your community. Perhaps there is someone who needs a visit by a neighbor, or would enjoy receiving some homemade cookies.

Here are some ways to show gratitude to God and your parents:

- Thank Jesus every day for your health and your ability to talk and walk and run.
- Thank Jesus every morning and night for each day you are given.
- Be thankful for your parents, and for any brothers and sisters you have.
- Be grateful for what you have. Don't be looking for more.
- Whenever someone gives you something, say "Thank you."
- Share what you have with others.

## Did You Know?

St. Martin of Tours is another saint who understood that Jesus wants us to help those in need. This became very real for Martin after he gave half of his red cloak to a poor, cold beggar. When Martin went to sleep that night, he had a dream. In his dream, Jesus was surrounded by angels, and Jesus was wearing the very same red cloak that Martin had given the beggar!

Also, did you know that grateful people are often healthier than ungrateful people? Grateful people tend to have a peaceful heart, knowing all things come from God. They don't worry as much as ungrateful people. Grateful people sleep better, which is good for their health. Grateful people often have more energy for exercising, and they even eat healthier. So, if you would like a head start on being healthy and happy, be grateful!

# Chapter 12. Respect for Others and Their Belongings

"Daddy, Tommy won't give me my plane back after I let him play with it," declared Annie.

"Tommy, though you are only three, you need to learn to give things back to those to whom they belong!" declared Father.

"Father, I think it is time that you talk with all the children about the meaning of owning and borrowing!" said Mother. "It isn't just Tommy who does not understand the difference!"

"This might be a good time to have a family meeting," Father agreed. "The children cannot go outside because it is cold and raining. On days like this, sometimes the children cannot seem to settle down."

Father then went around the house and explained what he wanted.

"Okay, Children," commanded Father, "It is time that we have a little family meeting about respect for others and their belongings! Let's all gather in the family room!"

One by one, the Martin children came into the family room and settled down on the chairs and the floor. Tommy brought his new red wagon to sit in.

"Thank you for coming so quietly and patiently for this family meeting, Children. Mother thinks we need a little discussion on the meaning of respecting what belongs to others," explained Father.

"This is my wagon, Dad," said Tommy. "I don't think Johnny should use it! He might break it!"

"Well, that is what we are here to talk about, Tommy!" continued Father, "Theresa, could you please explain what it means when we borrow something?"

"Okay, Dad. It means that what we borrow does not belong to us, and we must return it to the owner as soon as possible after we use it."

"I know," said Joanie, "that when I borrow something, I can use it, but I must return it when I am finished using it."

"Yes," jumped in Johnny, "but it also means that we must return the borrowed thing when the owner wants us to return it!"

"You are right about that, Johnny," said Mother. "When we borrow a library book, the library tells us the date when the book must be returned."

"When I borrow something from my girl friends, they tell me when I need to give it back to them," said Theresa. "And when I loan them something—when they borrow something from me—I tell them when I want it back."

"Perhaps," said Father, "we need to think about the Seventh Commandment, which says we must not steal. If we borrow something and don't return it on time, it's as if we have stolen it during the time we should not have it. Of course, if we don't return it at all, that really is stealing. Sometimes we think we will return it someday, and then we forget about it. But that is still stealing, in a way, even if it is due to our being forgetful!"

"There is something else we should think about, Father," said Mother. "When we return a borrowed item, it should be in exactly the same condition as when it was given to us. No part of it should be broken. No part of it should be different from the way it was when it was given to us."

"I remember," said Theresa, "that Father Johnson said we must respect what belongs to others, even if we don't borrow it. Father said that if we break something that belongs to someone else, we are commanded by the Seventh Commandment to fix it!"

"I remember Father Johnson saying that!" exclaimed Joanie. "Father said that, if it cannot be fixed, then we must offer to either buy another one to replace it or give the person the money it is worth. Otherwise, Father said, it is like stealing!"

"Johnny, do you remember what happened the other day at the library?" asked Mother.

"Yes, Mom," answered Johnny. "When I was reaching for a book on a high shelf, the book crashed down to the floor! You said I must be careful that I do not damage books! If I do damage a book, then I need to be prepared to give the library enough money to buy a new book. The librarian also told me that when I turn the pages of the library books, I should turn them carefully so that I don't tear the pages."

"You children have heard my stories about when I was a student in a Catholic school," reminded Mother. "The teachers, who were nuns, had special rules for us about how books were to be treated."

"We were required," Mother said, "to make book covers for all our books, and our hands had to be clean before we could touch a book. We were not allowed to mark the books with a pen or pencil either. The wise nuns taught us that good books are like jewels of knowledge. Books should be handled very carefully."

"Mother is right, Children, "Father declared. "Whether we handle a book or anything else borrowed from someone, we must treat it with extra care so that it can be returned in good condition. In fact, it would be better, if possible, that we not borrow anything that belongs to others."

"Father," Mother began, "There was one famous person who borrowed books from his neighbors. But he was known and much

Health 3 for Young Catholics

appreciated because he always returned the books he borrowed, even when he was a little boy!"

"Yes, Mother, you are right about that! Do any of you children remember who that famous person was?"

"I think I know whom you are talking about, Dad," replied Theresa. "Are you thinking about Abraham Lincoln?"

"Yes, Theresa, I'm glad you remember our famous president who was so poor as a boy that he needed to borrow books to read. But people happily loaned them to him because he returned them as soon as he read them. Those were in the days when there were no cars, and he walked to their homes to return their books!"

"The important thing to remember, Children," said Mother, "is what Jesus told us: Do unto others as you would have them do unto you! So let's be careful when we borrow something. Don't use something in a way that might end up breaking it! If that happens, you will need to buy another one for the person who owns it!"

"Last Christmas," said Johnny, "I remember when someone played with my new airplane. When someone played with it, it crashed and got broken!"

"I do remember that unhappy incident, Johnny!" Father said. "Someone had to gather up his allowance money and pay for another airplane for you! It is a matter of justice to pay for a replacement for anything we break that belongs to someone else!"

"What about litter, Dad?" asked Joanie. "There is a sign I saw on the road about not littering! I know Bobby's house is on the corner, and he said that when people throw empty bottles on his lawn, they aren't respecting his family's property!"

"Joanie, you bring up a good point," Father declared. "Being careful not to litter is not only a matter of respecting the property of others; it is also a matter of keeping other families healthy. In fact, it is really a matter of keeping the entire community healthy. We almost always talk about keeping healthy in our family, and we talk about keeping our house free of germs, but we usually don't think about keeping our neighborhood clean of litter and trash."

"Littering, throwing trash or garbage anywhere," explained Mother, "is not only showing disrespect for the property of others; it is also showing a lack of concern for the health of others in our neighborhood!"

"When the firemen talked to us at the fire station," Joanie reminded everyone, "they spoke about the dangers of littering. They said fires can start from litter! The firemen said that when people litter with food and garbage, it attracts animals, especially bears, to their property! And animals can be dangerous for children!"

"Littering," declared Father, "is also against the Seventh Commandment because it shows disrespect for the property of others. It is in a way stealing the good condition of a person's property. It is, in fact, showing disrespect for God's creation!"

"I remember seeing some little children throwing candy wrappers outside their car," declared Little Annie.

"I've seen that too!" exclaimed Johnny.

"I've seen signs that say not to throw trash in the river!" said Theresa.

"Throwing trash in the river is definitely showing disrespect for the beautiful world that God has given us to enjoy!" declared Mother. "When people do that, they not only are stealing people's right to enjoy the river; they also may be taking away the community's ability to have clean drinking water."

"You're right, Mother," declared Father. "Littering shows disrespect for God's creation, for the animals and the plants, for the fish, and even for people who need to drink clean water. It shows a disregard for God's world, His creatures, and His people."

"In conclusion," declared Father, "let's all agree to respect the property of others when we borrow things, and let's agree to have respect for the land and creatures that God has given us. Let's agree to do our best to keep healthy ourselves, and to keep our land and water safe for all people to remain healthy. God expects us to be good caretakers of the world He has given us, and of the people in our family and in our community."

## Lesson Review

1. Which Commandment tells us to respect the property of others?

   _____

2. How should we handle library books?

   _____

3. What might happen if a book is dropped too many times?

   _____

4. How did Abraham Lincoln show respect for the property of others?

   _____

J.M.J.

5. Name some examples of litter.

_____

_____

## Activities

*Clean-Up Time!*
Go on a trash hunt, either in your house, in the family car, or outside. (Ask your mom or dad for permission first!) See how many pieces of trash you can find to throw away. Make sure you wear work gloves and wash your hands when you are finished. If you have more time, search for things that are out of place. Put them where they belong. Your parents will be happy for your help in keeping things tidy!

*Reading the Bookshelves*
Spend some time organizing your books. Look at the books on a bookshelf one at a time. You do not need to take them off the shelf. Look to see if each book has its spine facing outward so that you can see the title. Also, check to make sure each book is right side up. If a book is not the right way, change it so that it is. Make sure no books are lying flat on top of the others. You and your family will enjoy seeing your bookshelf straightened out so nicely!

> "The sinner shall borrow, and not pay again;
> but the just shows mercy and shall give." (Psalm 36:21)

## Did You Know?

The Library of Congress in Washington, D.C., is the largest library in the world. There are more than 30 million books there!

# Chapter 13. Good Posture

The Martin family took a trip to the National Zoo while they were visiting Washington, D.C. They spent the day looking at the animals from all over the world. On their way back in the car to the hotel, the Martin children talked about the many animals they saw at the zoo.

"So, Tommy, which animals did you like seeing the best?" asked Mother.

"I liked the lions and the tigers the best," exclaimed Tommy loudly.

"Yes," Father chuckled. "They walked so proudly, like they own the zoo!"

"I liked the monkeys," yelled Annie. "They are so funny! And they swing around and around, from one side to the other, swinging and swinging and swinging!"

"Well, I don't know if I actually liked the alligators and snakes, but it was neat to see them," declared Johnny. "But the elephants were fantastic! The sign said that the smallest elephant was over 4,000 pounds! They would swing their trunks this way and that way, and, while standing in the water, they would shoot water out of their trunks! But I would not want to get near an elephant! They are awfully big!"

"I think I liked the zebras the best," said Joanie. "They are so beautiful and elegant and colorful!"

"The giraffes are so unusual, Mom," said Theresa. "They hold up their long necks so high! They must have very strong backs. How do they keep their long necks so straight?"

"God gave them those long necks and strong backs so that they can eat the leaves off the highest trees. The other animals eat the leaves off the lower branches," Dad responded.

"Standing as straight and tall as we can is important for all of us, especially boys and girls as they are growing up," said Mother, "just as it is important for giraffes. Good posture is the habit of standing and sitting straight and tall."

"Good posture is something we have not talked about much lately, Children," declared Father. "Maybe now, while we are driving home, this might be a good time to talk about all of us keeping good posture!"

"The most important point to think about regarding good posture is to stand straight. We can do this by keeping in mind that we want to stand tall, and not slouch at all!" explained Mother.

"Standing tall and straight is probably the best and shortest reminder to help us have healthy posture," replied Father. "What many people don't realize is that if we don't stand straight and tall, we will not stay healthy. We need to have good posture so that we can have good health!"

"Another idea for standing straight," suggested Mother, "is to keep looking straight ahead. Keep your shoulders back too. There is no need to be looking down, unless you are going up or down the stairs!"

"To tell you the truth, Mother, I don't see the children slouching when they are walking. I see too much slouching when they are sitting!" stated Father. "I suppose slouching is more comfortable when you are reading, but you surely don't want to stay in that position for long. It could influence your standing posture over a period of time."

"Dad, when I went to those ballet classes last year, the teacher recommended an idea for sitting correctly," remembered Theresa. "She told us that to practice good posture while we are sitting, we should find a ball that is the size of a tennis ball. Then put the ball between our back and the back of the chair. While we are sitting, we should keep the ball from falling by pressing our back against it. This will help us to sit correctly in a chair."

"I don't know, Mother, whether this is a good idea or not," suggested Joanie, "but when I went to help out at that fundraiser for the lady who was sick in our parish, we had that fashion show to raise money."

"Yes, I remember, Joanie. You wore a beautiful green dress with white lace on the sleeves!" declared Mother.

"Well," continued Joanie, "when the director was telling us how to walk to show off our dress, she said we should imagine that we have a helium balloon attached to the top of our head. She said to imagine that the balloon is pulling us up straight. She said that thinking like that was a good way to keep our backs straight while we were walking to show off our dresses!"

"That sounds like a great idea, Joanie," declared Father. "Certainly, practicing good posture helps you to breathe better too. When your body is straight, you can take big, deep breaths. Then your lungs will fill up and the air will pass into the other parts of your body and into your blood where it is needed. When you are running and playing outdoors, you are taking deep breaths without noticing it. Good posture helps with proper breathing, so it helps to keep us healthy!"

"Being active and exercising also helps improve posture," said Mother. "Exercising makes your bones and muscles stronger, which helps you to stand straighter. We have talked before about the importance of eating foods with calcium and vitamin D. Well, calcium and vitamin D, which you get from milk, will help build your bones as well. Good bones will help with good posture, and good posture helps you to have good health."

"It is obvious that God has shown us how to have good health and good posture," declared Father.

"What about good posture at church, Dad?" asked Johnny. "I noticed a lot of people in church do not have good posture during Mass! Are they tired, Dad?"

"I don't know why sometimes people don't have good posture at Mass. But we need to think about this: when we are at church," began Father, "our posture says something about what we think is happening at Mass and about what we believe when we are praying."

Health 3 for Young Catholics

"When you are sitting, it is time for listening and thinking about what is being prayed. Standing shows respect for the prayers or words spoken. Kneeling shows adoration for God, especially as the miracle of the Holy Eucharist is taking place. We need to hold our bodies straight as we sit, kneel, or stand. There's an old Catholic saying: "As we pray, so we believe; as we believe, so we pray,"" Father said.

"One thing I have noticed," said Mother, "is that sometimes little ones lean on the pew or tend to play in the pew. Little Annie and Tommy need to be reminded about not leaning on the pew or playing on the kneeler. Even you little ones must be showing God that you love Him, and you should ask Him to help you to be good. You want to show God that you love Him, especially when you are in church at Mass."

"When we pray at home, either in our bedrooms or in front of our living room altar," began Theresa, "I know, Mother, that you and Dad are reminding us that we all must have good prayer posture on our knees and not be playing around during our Rosary. Sometimes when we go to our weekly neighborhood Rosary group, some parents need to remind their children to kneel quietly and not play around."

"I kneel next to my bed when I say my prayers!" claimed little Annie.

"Your good kneeling posture, Annie," said Mother, "shows that you are trying your best for Jesus."

"Well, here we are at our hotel!" exclaimed Father. "We had a good time at the zoo! And we were inspired by the animals God gave us to visit! We also had a good lesson on posture. Now we can go in and have a little something to eat, and then say our Rosary before bedtime."

## Lesson Review

1. How can you practice having good posture while sitting?

   _____

   _____

2. What can you imagine is at the top of your head that will help your posture?

   _____

3. Does good posture help you to breathe better?

   _____

4. How does exercise help your posture?

   _____

   _____

5. Name a time when you should have good prayer posture.

   _____

   _____

## Activities

*Posture Exercises*

Try these exercises to help you to have better posture:

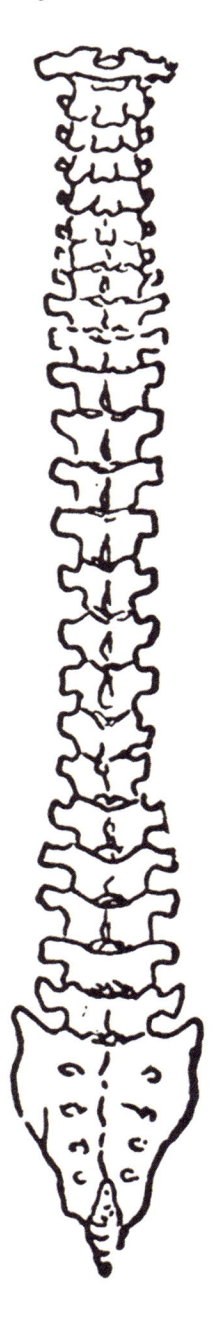

- Find a nice, flat hard-cover book. While standing, place it on your head. See how far you can walk without letting the book fall.
- Sit on a chair. Stretch your back, as though you were trying to touch your shoulder blades together. Hold this stretch for 10 seconds.
- Find a nice, clear wall in your house. Stand with your back against the wall. Now, make wall angels! Wave your arms up and down, sliding them against the wall. Keep your arms straight while you wave them. This is a good stretch for your back.

"And He laid His hands upon her, and immediately she was made straight, and glorified God." (Luke 13:13)

## Did You Know?

The vertebrae are the sections of bone that make your backbone. A giraffe has seven of these in its long neck—and so do you!

# Chapter 14. Household Health and Safety

"Mom," Annie ran in the house to tell her mother, "Tommy just fell off his tricycle out in the driveway! He was not wearing his helmet!"

"Oh, dear, he must have run out when I was upstairs. Look for Dad while I go out and get Tommy!"

Mother went out and found Tommy sitting in the driveway. "I bumped my head, Mom!" Tommy said slowly.

"Okay, Tommy. I am going to pick you up and carry you inside to the family room, where you can rest on the couch!"

Mother picked up Tommy, carried him inside, and laid him on the couch in the family room.

J.M.J.

Dad came into the room and said, "Tommy, I hear you fell off your bike, and you were not wearing your helmet. Do you have a headache?"

"A little one, Dad," Tommy answered weakly.

"Okay, Tommy, you just stay there and rest. Mother, I think you should stay here and watch Tommy for a while. Did you check his eyes to see if he has a concussion?"

"No, I didn't," she answered, "but I can do that now." Mother looked closely in Tommy's eyes.

"Why are you looking in my eyes, Mom?" asked Tommy.

"I need to make sure your pupils are not dilated, or bigger than normal. That might mean you have a concussion."

"How do his eyes look, Mother!" Father asked.

"His pupils seem to be normal, but I will sit with him a while and keep checking them," responded Mother.

Joanie and Johnny ran into the room. "What happened to Tommy?"

"He fell off his bike," Mother answered.

"Should we pray for him, Mom?" asked Joanie.

"Very definitely, Joanie. You and Johnny go outside on the porch swing and say some prayers for Tommy that he does not have a concussion."

"Okay, Mom."

J.M.J.

"Well, Mother, I can see that tomorrow I need to have a family meeting to discuss outdoor safety, and also indoor safety," stated Father. "It seems like we need to talk about these things every once in a while, because the children forget about them if we don't remind them again and again."

The next day, Sunday afternoon, after Mass and after everyone had eaten lunch, Dad called the family together for a meeting in the family room.

"Here we are again, Children, to discuss something important: household health and safety!" declared Father. "Tommy seems to have recovered from his fall, but he did not obey the rule about wearing his helmet when he was riding his tricycle!"

"I'm sorry, Dad," Tommy said weakly.

"Okay, Tommy! Well, Mother, it looks like just about everyone is here: Theresa, Joanie, Johnny, Annie, and Tommy. Rosie is taking her nap upstairs!" declared Dad.

"Father, let's start with talking about outside activities, proper exercise, and safety tips, since our meeting is the result of an outside activity!" said Mother.

"Okay, Mother. Well, Theresa," started Father, "since you are the oldest, would you like to start talking about rules regarding sports and exercise outside the house?"

"Sure, Dad!" agreed Theresa. "The first rule we all know about is that we need to wear a helmet when we ride our bicycles, or tricycles. The police say it is a law! And you want us to wear our helmets also when we roller skate on the sidewalk! And I know you like us to wear a helmet when we go ice skating at the skating rink! And a few Sundays ago, when I was on the skateboard, you told me that it is the law for me to wear a helmet when I am skateboarding!"

Health 3 for Young Catholics

J.M.J.

"Children don't realize how often they can get seriously hurt when they don't wear helmets," emphasized Father. "In fact, over at the high school, all the boys must wear helmets when they play football! And the soccer players wear helmets as well."

"There are other sports in which we don't need to wear helmets," declared Joanie, "and I like to play those—like basketball, swimming, tennis, running, and just plain walking, especially in the park and in the woods!"

"That is a good point too," Mother said. "All kinds of exercise are important, for all of us, to stay healthy. So we do want to emphasize that all of us should be doing physical exercises every day to stay healthy. But we also want to stay safe!"

"We do need to emphasize the importance of daily exercise," declared Father. "Daily exercise is essential for stronger muscles and bones. We cannot be healthy and strong without daily exercise. Daily exercise also helps keep us from becoming overweight. Daily exercise helps us from getting various diseases that can result from lack of exercise. The fact is that daily exercise, especially outside in the fresh air, makes us feel good and feel happy!"

"I notice," added Theresa, "that if I exercise after lunch, I can do my afternoon lessons better. I don't get sleepy or lazy!"

"Well," admitted Mother, "I sometimes watch the early morning exercises on the television, and I try to keep up with the ladies and their exercises. Although I find it difficult at the time, I notice my muscles and joints seem to feel better afterward. I can move better and even stretch better and farther after doing the exercises!"

"The doctor told me that when we exercise," submitted Dad, "our hearts beat faster, and that strengthens the heart. And when we breathe harder, the body is more able to deliver oxygen to all the body's cells, all of which makes us feel better!"

"Let's talk about preventing accidents at home," suggested Mother.

"That is a good idea, Mother!" agreed Father. "Two places where accidents occur the most in a home are the bathroom and the kitchen. Joanie, would you like to make some suggestions?"

"Things I know we need to watch out for are anything sharp or electric," noted Joanie. "In fact, Theresa and I don't use the hair dryer in the bathroom, but in our bedroom, so that there is no chance of the plug getting wet, and so that the little ones won't play with it."

"That is a good point, Joanie," noted Mother, "and it reminds me that anything sharp should be kept in the high medicine cabinet. Also, Father and I keep our medications on the highest shelf in the cabinet. I keep all my cosmetics, cleaners, perfumes, and all kinds of cleaning sprays and liquids high up in the clothes closet and the towel closet. I know that the little ones cannot reach those high shelves. And they know that those items are dangerous."

"Yes, Mom," said Annie. "You told me and Tommy about that."

"Joanie, would you like to say something about safety in the kitchen?" asked Father.

"Well, Mom has been keeping the sharp utensils, especially the knives, up on a shelf above the sink. That way, the younger children cannot reach them. In fact, I can't reach them either!"

"That's right, Joanie. I keep only the serving spoons and other safe kitchen items in the lower drawers!" answered Mother. "And I keep all the kitchen cleaners and detergents, matches, and everything that could be dangerous, in the utility closet. There is a semi-lock on that door; it can be

Health 3 for Young Catholics

pulled open, but only with extra strength. That means that no one, without permission, may use those items!"

"One thing we don't think about as being dangerous," began Father, "is the garbage. But the garbage can spread disease. So we have the garbage in a garbage can, but we have put it in the back room by the back door. That keeps it away from the little ones, and it also keeps the air clean in the house. However, I take the garbage to the local garbage-disposal place almost every day on my way to work. Some people leave their garbage outside, and that attracts animals, which can be dangerous to children."

"The other day," said Theresa, "when I visited grandmother's house, she had some kitchen shelves redone for a utility closet. She took out some lower shelves, and she put the garbage can inside the closet. It's really cool! You cannot see it or smell it!"

"I was just thinking, Dad," said Johnny, "about phone numbers. We talked about 911, but maybe I should know other phone numbers too!"

"Now you are thinking, Johnny!" proclaimed Dad. "Let's think about other phone numbers that everyone should know. And perhaps we can write these numbers on a bulletin board in the kitchen, in the hallway, and in the bathroom upstairs! Sometimes when there is an emergency, we cannot remember phone numbers! In fact, we should put a list of phone numbers in the car and maybe, Mother, you can put the list in your purse!"

"I can type out all the numbers on the computer," offered Joanie. "I can even print them out in color!"

"Would it be a good idea to put the emergency numbers in the cell phones too, Mom?" asked Theresa.

"That is a great idea, Theresa!" declared Father.

"We should include the poison control center," Mother suggested, "as well as the police and fire department numbers. Perhaps we should put the doctor's number on the list too. And we should put Dad's cell phone number on my cell phone, and put mine on his! We should also include grandma and grandpa's phone number!"

"Well, we have accomplished a lot at this family meeting!" said Father seriously." So, I am glad we had this meeting. But, Tommy, I hope you learned your lesson about the importance of wearing your helmet when you ride your bike!"

"Yes, Dad," Tommy answered. "But for my birthday, can you buy me a red helmet?"

"Meeting dismissed," declared Father abruptly.

## Lesson Review

1. What is the emergency phone number in the country where you live?

   _____

2. Name the two places in the home where accidents occur most often.

   _____

Health 3 for Young Catholics

3. List some of the times when children should wear a helmet.

   _____

   _____

4. List two things that should be kept on a high shelf.

   _____

5. Name three benefits of daily exercise.

   _____

   _____

6. Write down the following phone numbers.

   Police Station: _____

   Fire Department: _____

   Dad's Cell Phone: _____

   Mom's Cell Phone: _____

## Activities

1. Go with your parents to the police station, fire department, or doctor's office and pick up some free brochures about safety in the home.

2. On large construction paper (which you can find in the art department at local stores), make a poster about Fire Safety Rules.

3. Ask Mom or Dad to take you to a store to look at rope ladders for children to escape from a fire on the second floor.

# Chapter 15. First Aid

"Mom! Mom! Johnny cut his arm!" yelled Joanie running in the kitchen door.

Mom came running from the living room. "Okay, Joanie, where is he?"

"He is walking slowly, but he is coming in the yard now!"

"Joanie, go out with him while I get the First Aid Kit!"

Joanie ran outside. In just a few minutes, Johnny came walking in, holding his arm high, with a large cut underneath his arm.

"Well, Johnny," said Mom calmly, "sit over here by the table so that I can see your wound and wash it carefully! Let me take a clean gauze pad out of the First Aid Kit so that I can wash it clean."

"It really hurts, Mom!"

"I will give you an aspirin later, Johnny. Right now, I need to wash the cut and put a bandage on it!"

"It hurts, Mom!"

"Hold still, Johnny! Rest your arm on the table here so that I can clean the area to see where the cut is and how deep it is. Maybe you will need stitches!"

"Ouch!"

"Hold still, Johnny. While I am helping you, you should be saying prayers to thank God that you are not worse, and you should pray that I can fix your arm quickly. I am using just warm water. I need to clean it up so that I can see where the cut is?"

"Should I say prayers for Johnny, Mom?" asked Annie.

"Yes, Annie. That would be perfect. Please find Tommy, and you both can go in the family room and say a Rosary for Johnny!"

Annie ran to find Tommy to say the Rosary.

"Do I need stitches, Mom?"

"Well, it does not look too deep, Johnny. Let me put a little antiseptic on it. There. Now I will put a bandage on it to pull the edges together. Okay! Now I am going to put a larger gauze on it and tape around the gauze."

"Were you a nurse, Mom?" asked Joanie.

"No," Mother responded, "but I did take a First Aid course."

"Well, Mom, with Johnny around, maybe we should all take a First Aid course! Remember last summer when he cut his leg? And remember the time he cut his finger on a knife in the kitchen?"

"Johnny, I will get you something to help you with the pain. I do not think you need to see a doctor. But we will keep an eye on it, and if it does not heal quickly, we can see the doctor."

Just then, Father entered the kitchen.

"What is going on here, Mother?"

"Johnny cut his arm, Dad!" declared Joanie. "But Mom thinks that he will be okay."

"Well, I'm glad he will be okay. But I can see it is time for another family meeting about First Aid! I think we have had three First Aid meetings already, because of Johnny's accidents!"

"He is just an active boy, Father," Mother responded, "but we do need to emphasize to the children that they should not take risks or do things that could be dangerous to their health!"

Health 3 for Young Catholics

"After dinner, let's have a family meeting and talk about the importance of staying safe, as well as what to do in case of accidents. Theresa attended that First Aid class at the fire department last year. She can help us talk about how to take care of ourselves and others in an accident."

Later, after dinner, Father called the children into the family room for a discussion about First Aid.

"First, Children," began Father, "before we begin, let's say an Our Father to thank God that Johnny was not badly hurt and that Mom was able to fix him up without having to take him to the hospital."

After the family said the Our Father, Dad said, "You all know we have a First Aid Kit. Everyone here knows where we keep the First Aid Kit on the lower shelf in the kitchen. It is available to everyone except Tommy and Rosie, since they are too young to use it."

"Why do we keep the First Aid Kit in the kitchen?" asked Annie.

"The kitchen is the most likely place for an accident to occur," stated Father, "because of sharp knives, possible burns from the stove, and appliances that could possibly cause accidents. Even a mixer could hurt someone who puts his fingers too close! As you know, we also keep a fire extinguisher in the kitchen!"

"And in the kitchen, I have running water to wash cuts and wounds," declared Mother, "so it is handy to have the First Aid Kit in the kitchen.

"What do we keep in the First Aid Kit?" asked Father. "Does anyone know?"

"Well, let's take a look," said Mother. "I brought the kit in here so that we can take a look."

"Theresa, you took the course at the fire station," reminded Father. "Why don't you explain what is in the First Aid Kit!"

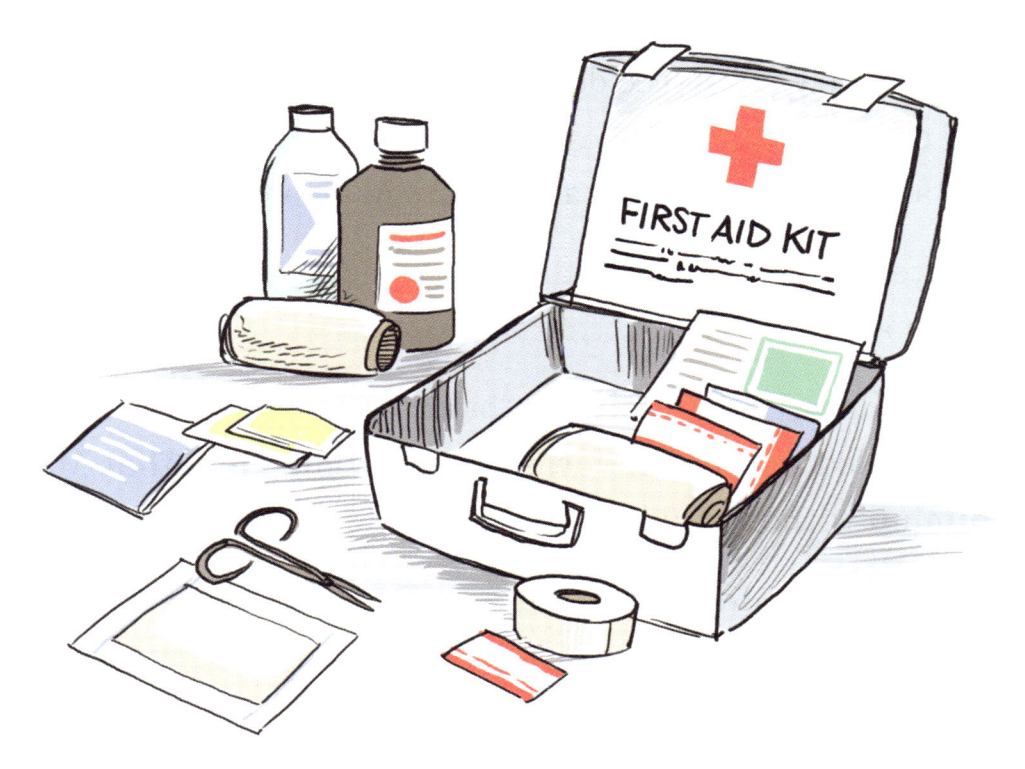

"The first thing is that they gave us an American Red Cross book called Standard First Aid and Personal Safety," Theresa said. "Here it is! Mom keeps it under the First Aid Kit."

"What does the book include?" Father asked.

"The chapters are on First Aid for wounds, for bleeding, and for prevention of contamination and infection. I remember the teacher emphasized keeping wounds clean to prevent infection. The book explains how to take care of different kinds of wounds. Remember when Johnny stepped on a nail in the garage? That is called a puncture wound!"

"What did the book say to do if a cut or wound does not stop bleeding," asked Joanie.

"The first rule" said Theresa, "is to stop the bleeding by applying pressure. The book talks a lot about applying pressure. It says you can apply a clean cloth or a bandage first, but applying pressure is the first important thing to do, even if all you have is your hand. It is important to have something clean to wash the wound or to wrap up the wound. The teacher said that, in an emergency, a person could use his undershirt or some other piece of clean clothing if something that big is necessary."

"I remember in that bomb blast in Boston," Father said, "some men used their shirts to tightly wrap up the wounds where people were bleeding!"

"Does the book talk about how to take care of a cut on someone's arm?" asked Johnny.

"Yes, the book covers all kinds of wounds," explained Theresa. "It gives suggestions about different sorts of injuries, such as head and neck injuries, back injuries, and injuries in all parts of the body. It also includes things like blisters, choking, poisoning, burns, frostbite, and fainting!"

"I remember the girl that fainted in church at her First Holy Communion last year," declared Joanie.

"Yes," Mother said. "Sometimes young children cannot go a long time without having something to eat, and that Mass went very long because there were so many children in the First Holy Communion class!"

"Theresa, can you tell us what is contained in the First Aid Kit?" asked Father.

"Well, Father, you purchased the large-size kit, I guess because we have such a large family. But I noticed at some stores, they have plenty of smaller kits for small families or to fit in the car."

"It seems like we have a lot in that First Aid Kit!" said Johnny.

"This First Aid Kit is pretty cool!" said Theresa. "It has a top section you can clip off like this, and it contains every size and shape of bandage you can buy! In addition, it contains safety pins, tweezers, a shaver with a razor blade, and a thermometer."

"What is in the bottom part of the kit?" asked Joanie.

"In the bottom of the kit is every kind and size, both small and large, of bandages, or I should say gauze pads. There is also a bottle of pain-relieving cleansing spray. Maybe Mom used that on your wound, Johnny! There is a folded-up emergency blanket; when people get injured, they often get chilled very quickly, because their body is suffering from shock! There is a junior and adult-size splint in the kit! There is a large blood-stopper dressing! There are masks in case of fire or gas in the air. There is eyewash. And there is a kit for the rescue person to clean up himself in case he has blood or other fluids that might be poisonous or dangerous to his health!"

"That is great, Theresa," Father said. "Thank you for telling us all about what is in the kit! After our meeting, let's spread out all the items on the table, so that everyone is familiar with what we have and how it should be used!"

"Wow!" said Johnny. "I guess no matter what happens to me, there is something in that kit to fix me up!"

"Well, Johnny Boy," demanded Father, "I don't want you to take chances any more! And especially, Tommy, you need to stop standing on a chair to reach something! I would prefer that we never need to open that First Aid Kit!"

"I wonder if I would know what to use in the kit, Dad," said Joanie.

"What we need to do, Mother," said Father, "is phone the fire department or the hospital and find out when they will be teaching the next First Aid course. We should send Joanie and Johnny if they are old enough for the class. Then maybe Johnny could take care of himself the next time he falls, right Johnny?"

"The other thing, Children, is this," said Mother. "Stay close to home. Don't wander too far about the neighborhood. If you should get hurt or fall off your bike, or whatever, you need to come home quickly so that we can help you! Of course, if you are not too close to home, you could ask someone you know where you are."

Health 3 for Young Catholics

J.M.J.

"Yes," agreed Father. "And if you are in someone else's home, be sure to find the nearest adult for help! You should not be in someone's home without an adult being present!"

"If there is no adult around," Father said, " try to phone 911 or ask someone else to phone the number. That is the emergency phone number. The police can send help, and perhaps send an ambulance. I know that you all know the 911 number. Tommy, even you should know that, although you are only three years old. If there is an emergency and you need help, dial 911 on the phone."

"Last week," Father began, "there was a boy about seven years old. A strange man came into the house. No adult was home, which was not right, of course. But the boy went into the bathroom with a cell phone, locked the door, and dialed 911. He was able to give his address in a whisper, and the person he talked to actually gave the address to the police. The police came out immediately and captured the man. You children need to be quick-thinking in case of trouble. And you need to pray a lot in dangerous situations."

"Let's say a prayer right now," suggested Mother, "to thank Jesus that Johnny was not seriously hurt, and to ask Him to please keep everyone in our family holy, happy, healthy, and safe! Jesus has been very good to our family, and we need to thank Him!"

## Lesson Review

1. What is the first thing to do when someone has a cut?

_____

_____

Health 3 for Young Catholics

2. What is usually contained in a First Aid Kit?

_____

_____

_____

_____

3. What phone number do you need to remember in case of an accident?

_____

4. What are some things you should not do, so that you can stay safe?

_____

_____

_____

## Activities

With your mom or dad, look over the things in your family's First Aid Kit. Become familiar with how the different things would be used.

**Parent:** Consider having your child take a First Aid course at a local hospital or fire department. Usually, there is only one meeting date for the lesson. Also, there are free lessons and further information for First Aid courses on the Internet.

J.M.J.

# Chapter 16. Courtesy at Church

Like many Catholic families, the Martins start each day by attending Holy Mass at their nearby church. One Saturday, when they returned home, Mother started talking to the children about courtesy at church.

"You children were very good at Mass this morning," she began. "We need to make the beds and do a little cleaning, but while we do, I want to talk with you about going to Mass."

"We know about going to Mass, Mama!" exclaimed Tommy.

"Yes, Tommy, but did you know," Mother explained, "that, in many places in the world, there are not enough priests, and people may need to walk miles to attend a church, even on Sundays?"

Mr. Martin walked into Tommy's bedroom. "I heard your mother, Tommy, "and what she says is true!"

"Well," said Johnny as he continued making his bed, "we need to pray for all those people, that there will be more priests there!"

"That's true, Johnny," said Father, "and we need to thank Jesus that we can attend Mass and receive Jesus every morning."

"While we realize it is a great blessing to be able to receive Jesus each morning at Mass," stated Mother, "we also need to show Jesus how much we thank Him for giving us this great blessing. One way we can show our thanks to Jesus is to dress nicely and neatly when we attend Mass. We don't want to wear clothes that are not clean and neat."

Joanie came into the room with Theresa. "We always wear our best clothes on Sunday," Joanie said. "We even wipe our shoes clean if they are dirty."

"Well, I do that, for me and for Tommy," said Johnny, rather slowly.

"I know that is sometimes hard to remember, Boys," began Father, "but we need to remember that, next to the angels, we are God's highest creatures."

"Jesus suffered and died for us," Father said. "So, to show our love for Jesus, we should express our thanks to Him by, among other things, being neat and tidy in our appearance at Mass."

"By the way, Tommy," Mother began, as she started cleaning the bathroom sink, "when you were leaving the church this morning, I noticed you started playing with the holy water. I think you even sprayed a little on Rosie!"

"Baby Rosie liked it, Mommy!"

"Well, Tommy, we don't do that," Mother said. "We dip only the tips of our fingers in the holy water font, and then we bless ourselves by making the Sign of the Cross with our wet fingers. Holy water is very special blessed water. It must never be splashed or played with. The water is holy because it has been given a special blessing by a priest. Holy water is a sacramental, like a rosary or a scapular. If it is treated with respect, it can help us to be good."

"Annie," Mother continued, "I noticed you did not genuflect before you entered the pew. You are a big enough girl now to know what to do. Before we enter the pew, we must genuflect on the right knee. Do you want to practice it now?"

"Okay, Mom!"

"I'll practice it with you, Annie!" said Johnny. Annie and Johnny practiced genuflecting three times.

"That's great, Annie! Johnny is a good teacher. Johnny, if you see Annie forget to genuflect, you help her to remember how to do it!"

"I will, Mom!"

Father entered the room again. "I heard you all talking about genuflecting. Perhaps I need to remind everyone that, even if there is no Mass, anytime we pass the tabernacle where Jesus is truly present, we should genuflect. By genuflecting in front of the tabernacle, we show that we believe God, our King, is truly present there."

"Yes, Children," Mother agreed. "Remember when we were visiting in Cleveland and we went to the beautiful old church, Immaculate Conception Church? It was built during the Civil War. When we went in to visit the church, we all went first up to the front of the church, in front of the tabernacle, and knelt down in front of Jesus. It was like saying a special "Hello!" to Jesus, telling Him that we know He is there, and that we love Him. Only after we greeted Him that way did we look at all the beautiful stained glass windows and colorful statues."

Theresa and Joanie joined Mom and Dad and the rest of the family in the family room to straighten it up for the day.

"I heard you, Mother," said Joanie, "when you talked about Immaculate Conception Church. One thing we always do when we visit a church is to talk very quietly."

"That is right, Joanie," agreed Father. "That is because wherever Jesus is present is a holy place. It is not polite to talk out loud in church. Even if there are people in the pews, they are silent because, in their hearts, they are speaking to Jesus, and He listens and hears them all."

Health 3 for Young Catholics

As Mother and Theresa picked up the newspapers, Theresa said, "One thing I do very carefully: when we go into a pew, I put down the kneeler gently and quietly. Sometimes little children don't know how heavy it is, and they accidentally bang it down!"

"That's true, Theresa," answered Father. "We must kneel down on the kneeler right away and make the Sign of the Cross, and greet Jesus, because we have come to visit Him in His House, which is every Catholic church where He is truly present. Kneeling straight shows respect to Jesus. As we kneel, we may look at the tabernacle, the crucifix, or the Stations of the Cross, or we may bow our heads. We should fold our hands together in prayer."

"Mom, what is the best prayer to say when we visit a church?" asked Joanie.

"Jesus gave us a prayer, the Our Father," reminded Mother. "We should say that first. But, after that, we should tell Jesus that we love Him and that we want to be good because He created us and loves us."

"I know it is hard for you, Tommy and Annie," said Father, "since you have not learned to read yet. But we do have those little picture missals for you. Of course, at any time, you can simply listen to the prayers. I notice that you, Annie, are learning to answer the Mass prayers. That shows that you are paying attention and getting yourself ready for First Holy Communion."

"What is the holiest part of the Mass, Mom?" asked Joanie. "Someone was asking me, and I said it is when the priest changes the bread and wine into the Body and Blood of Our Lord Jesus Christ."

"You are correct about that, Joanie," said Father. "That part of the Mass is called the Consecration. During that holiest of times during the Mass, it is most important to pay the closest attention to what the priest is doing at the altar. As we watch and wait for Jesus to come, we should have our hands folded, we should kneel straight, and we should silently pray with all our heart. When the priest says the words of Jesus, "This is My Body," we fix our eyes on the Host, which has changed to His Body. Then when the priest says, "This is the Chalice of My Blood," we fix our eyes on the raised chalice, which now contains His Blood."

"Mom, do you remember when Sister Mary visited us last year?" asked Theresa. "She gave a talk to us girls and said that we needed to have holy manners when we walk up to receive Our Lord in Holy Communion. She said that, when we go to meet Jesus in Holy Communion, we should have our hands folded and our eyes lowered. She said we should not be looking around for our friends. We should not be turning around either, as that would be rude and impolite to Jesus, since we should be preparing in our hearts to welcome Him."

"Well, Theresa," Mother agreed, "Sister Mary was right about that!"

"Sister Mary said we could kneel or stand to receive Jesus!"

"That is correct, Theresa, but if we are standing to receive Jesus, we should genuflect or bow our heads before receiving Him. We can kneel, genuflect, or bow to show respect to our Heavenly King, Who loves us and created us."

"Also," reminded Mother, "we walk back to our pew with our hands folded and not looking around at other people or our friends. Then, we go quietly into our pew without genuflecting, since we are carrying Jesus within us."

"While we are in our pew after we receive Jesus," reminded Father, "we should speak to Jesus and say our usual prayers, and any special

Health 3 for Young Catholics

prayers for anyone who is sick or in some special need. While the Body of Jesus is in our mouth, we must pay attention only to Him. We must not look around for our friends. It would be rude to have Jesus present in us yet we are not paying attention to Him!"

"I remember last year," said Theresa, "when that Franciscan brother visited us. He did not wear regular shoes; he wore brown sandals. The brother said that we must have good manners in church, that our actions should show that we are respectful of Jesus, Who is Our God and Savior. He said our good actions will show others that we are considerate of them while they are saying their prayers. I wonder if that Franciscan brother is coming back!"

"I remember that brother," exclaimed Johnny. "He wore a brown robe and a white belt of rope. And I liked his brown sandals. Do you think he will come back again this year?"

"I don't know, Johnny," said Father, "but we can ask our pastor when we go to Mass tomorrow. Perhaps that brother can come back and visit us. Maybe we can even invite him to dinner."

"Wow!" exclaimed Johnny. "That would be cool!"

## Lesson Review

1. What kind of clothes should we wear to Sunday Mass?

   _____

2. Why is holy water special?

   _____

   _____

J.M.J.

3. What do we do before entering our pew?

_____

4. Who are we showing respect for when we kneel straight?

_____

5. Who should we be thinking about when we walk up to Holy Communion?

_____

## Activities

*Saints and the Mass*

Here are some saints who had a very special love for the Holy Eucharist and the Mass. Find out more about one or more of these saints:

- *St. Imelda.* Find out what happened to her while she was at Mass.
- *St. Padre Pio.* Find out why he sometimes cried while saying Mass.
- *St. Joseph of Cupertino.* Find out what special thing he did while saying Mass.

Your mother or father can look on the Internet to find pictures of the various habits of brothers and nuns in different religious orders. How many different colors are the habits worn by the different orders of brothers and nuns?

J.M.J.

## Did You Know?

There are many, many angels at every Mass. Angels are invisible because they have no bodies; they are totally spirit. They fill the church, and they surround the priest and help him. They adore God and pray for us. One priest believes there could be a thousand angels at each Mass. So, the next time you are at Mass, remember to ask all the invisible angels to pray for you and your family!

At one parish, there is a nun, a sister, who comes to visit the girls to talk to them about dressing modestly. One day when she came, the girls baked cookies for the sister as a way of saying "Thank you." Let's remember to thank those at our parish church who do so much to help us.

J.M.J.

# Health 3
## Answer Key

### Chapter 1
1. Morning Offering
2. Angel of God Prayer
3. They said their prayers, dressed, washed their faces and brushed their teeth, brushed their hair, made their beds, put away their nightgowns, and tidied up.
4. Ten hours
5. Answers may vary.
6. It keeps us healthy and energetic throughout the day.
7. Answers may vary.
8. Answers may vary.

### Chapter 2
1. So that it will be clean and not tangled.
2. He takes them off, wipes them on the mat, and puts them in a box.
3. Sunday
4. He takes it off and puts it in his pocket.
5. It keeps his shirt in place.
6. He wants to teach Tommy to be a good altar boy.

### Chapter 3
1. Because germs can enter your body through your eyes, nose, and mouth.
2. They can make you sick.
3. Wash your hands.
4. Answers may vary. Examples include hairbrushes, plates, cups and glasses, forks, spoons, napkins, and toothbrushes.
5. Answers may vary. See the previous page for examples.

### Chapter 4
1. Primary teeth
2. Permanent teeth
3. Thirty-two teeth
4. At bedtime
5. St. Apollonia
6. When they touch their eyes with dirty hands.
7. St. Lucy

### Chapter 5
1. No
2. The milk group
3. Answers may vary.
4. Dark green vegetables and brightly colored vegetables
5. Answers may vary.
6. Answers may vary.

### Chapter 6
1. Answers may vary.
2. Because your body uses a lot of water when you are exercising.
3. Yes
4. Good sportsmanship means having good manners in our games. That means playing fair and being nice to the other team, whether we win or lose. Win or lose, we should treat others the way we would like to be treated.
5. Answers may vary.
6. Answers may vary.
7. Answers may vary.
8. The Fourth Commandment
9. Answers may vary.

### Chapter 7
1. He might hurt himself or others.
2. In the house, in stores, and at church.
3. Because they might put the items in their mouth and choke.
4. Because someone could step on or stumble over them.
5. If you swallow medicine that is not for you, you could get sick and have to go to the hospital.

### Chapter 8
1. Smoke detectors, fire extinguishers, and fire escape ladders
2. Crawl on the floor and look for an exit.
3. Stop, drop, and roll.
4. Answers may vary.

### Chapter 9
1. So that you don't get lost.
2. Answers may vary. Examples include a policeman (if available), a worker with a name tag (while at a store or museum), or a mother with children.
3. Do not answer the stranger. Run away from the stranger and find Mom or Dad.
4. No
5. Answers may vary. Examples include the TV, video games, and the Internet.
6. Angel of God, my guardian dear, to whom God's love commits me here. Ever this day, be at my side, to light and guard, to rule and guide. Amen.

Health 3 for Young Catholics

### Chapter 10
1. Say grace.
2. On your lap
3. The guest began to eat without saying grace.
4. You should ask to be excused.
5. Answers may vary.

### Chapter 11
1. We should treat others in the same way that we would like to be treated.
2. God wants us to love all people.
3. She helped those in need.
4. Forgive them.
5. Answers may vary.
6. He wants us to do good for others, and to help one another.
7. It makes you feel good inside.
8. Answers may vary.
9. Answers may vary.
10. No
11. Answers may vary.

### Chapter 12
1. The Seventh Commandment
2. Very carefully
3. It might become damaged.
4. He always returned the books he borrowed.
5. Answers may vary.

### Chapter 13
1. Put a ball between your back and the chair. While you are sitting, keep the ball from falling by pressing your back against it.
2. A balloon
3. Yes
4. Exercising makes your bones and muscles stronger, which helps you to stand straighter.
5. We should have good prayer posture whenever we are at Mass or in church, while praying the Rosary, and any other time when we pray.

### Chapter 14
1. The answer depends on the country in which you live. The emergency number in the United States is 911.
2. The kitchen and the bathroom
3. Answers may vary. Examples include while riding a bicycle (or tricycle), roller skating, ice skating, skateboarding, playing football, and playing soccer.
4. Answers may vary. Examples include sharp utensils, medications, cosmetics, cleaners, perfumes, and anything else dangerous to little children.
5. Answers may vary. Examples include building stronger muscles and bones, helping us from becoming overweight, helping us from getting various diseases, and (especially outside in the fresh air) making us feel good and feel happy.
6. Answers may vary.

### Chapter 15
1. Stop the bleeding by applying pressure.
2. Answers may vary.
3. 911 (or whatever the emergency number is in the country where you live).
4. Answers may vary.

### Chapter 16
1. Clothes that are clean and neat
2. Because it has been given a special blessing by a priest.
3. Genuflect.
4. Jesus
5. Jesus

# Notes

## Notes

# Notes

# Like our books?

You might like our program too. Seton Home Study School offers a full curriculum program for Pre-Kindergarten through Twelfth Grade. We include daily lesson plans, answer keys, quarterly tests, and much more. Our staff of teachers and counselors is available to answer questions and offer help. We keep student records and send out diplomas that are backed by our accreditation with the AdvancEd Accreditation Commission.

For more information about Seton Home Study School, please contact our admissions office.

**Seton Home Study School
1350 Progress Drive
Front Royal, VA 22630**

Phone: 540-636-9990 • Fax: 540-636-1602
Internet: www.setonhome.org • E-mail: info@setonhome.org